Contents

Volume 14: Romans—Philippians   by Dorothy Jean Furnish

Introduction to the Series		2
Chapter 1	Being Human	3
Chapter 2	A Vision of Freedom	8
Chapter 3	Christians and Jews	13
Chapter 4	Discovering What Is Good	18
Chapter 5	Strange Wisdom	23
Chapter 6	Particular Gifts	28
Chapter 7	Necessary Knowledge	33
Chapter 8	Faith, Incorporated	38
Chapter 9	A New Creation	43
Chapter 10	Strength Through Weakness	48
Chapter 11	Children of Promise	53
Chapter 12	One New Humanity	58
Chapter 13	One Name Above All	63
Connected to One Another		68
Paul Speaks to "Sensible People"		70
Map: The World of Paul		Inside back cover

Introduction to the Series

The leader's guides provided for use with JOURNEY THROUGH THE BIBLE make the following assumptions:
- adults learn in different ways:
  —by reading
  —by listening to speakers
  —by working on projects
  —by drama and roleplay
  —by using their imaginations
  —by expressing themselves creatively
  —by teaching others
- the mix of persons in your group is different from that found in any other group;
- the length of the actual time you have for teaching in a session may vary from thirty minutes to ninety minutes;
- the physical place where your class meets is not exactly like the place where any other group or class meets;
- your teaching skills, experiences, and preferences are unlike anyone else's.

We encourage you to discover and develop the ways you can best use the information and learning ideas in this leader's guide with your particular class. To get started, we suggest you try following these steps:

1. Think and pray about your individual class members. Who are they? What are they like? Why are they involved in this particular Bible study class at this particular time in their lives? What seem to be their needs? How do you think they learn best?
2. Think and pray about your class members as a group. A group takes on a character that can be different from the particular characters of the individuals who make up that group. How do your class members interact? What do they enjoy doing together? What would help them become stronger as a group?
3. Keep in mind that you are teaching this class for the sake of the class members, in order to help them increase in their faithfulness as disciples of Jesus Christ. Teachers sometimes fall prey to the danger of teaching in ways that are easiest for themselves. The best teachers accept the discomfort of taking risks and stretching their teaching skills in order to focus on what will really help the class members learn and grow in their faith.
4. Read the chapter in the study book. Read the assigned Bible passages. Read the background Bible passages, if any. Work through the Dimension 1 questions in the study book. Make a list of any items you do not understand and need to research further using such tools as Bible dictionaries, concordances, Bible atlases, and commentaries. In other words, do your homework. Be prepared with your own knowledge about the Bible passages being studied by your class.
5. Read the chapter's material in the leader's guide. You might want to begin with the "Additional Bible Helps," found at the *end* of each chapter. Then look at each learning idea in the "Learning Menu."
6. Spend some time with the "Learning Menu." Notice that the "Learning Menu" is organized around Dimensions 1, 2, and 3 in the study book. Recognizing that different adults and adult classes will learn best using different teaching/learning methods, in each of the three dimensions you will find
   —at least one learning idea that is primarily discussion-based;
   —at least one learning idea that begins with a method other than discussion, but which may lead into discussion.

   Make notes about which learning ideas will work best given the unique makeup and setting of your class.
7. Decide on a lesson plan. Which learning ideas will you lead the class members through when? What materials will you need? What other preparations do you need to make? How long do you plan to spend on a particular learning idea?
8. Many experienced teachers have found that they do better if they plan more than they actually use during a class session. They also know that their class members may become frustrated if they try to do too much during a class session. In other words
   —plan more than you can actually use. That way, you have back-up learning ideas in case something does not work well or something takes much less time than you thought.
   —don't try to do everything listed in the "Learning Menu." We have intentionally offered you much more than you can use in one class session.
   —be flexible while you teach. A good lesson plan is only a guide for your use as you teach people. Keep the focus on your class members, not your lesson plan.
9. After you teach, evaluate the class session. What worked well? What did not? What did you learn from your experience of teaching that will help you plan for the next class session?

May God's Spirit be upon you as you lead your class on their *Journey Through the Bible*!

Questions or comments? Call Curric-U-Phone 1-800-251-8591

1 Being Human

Romans 3:21–4:25

LEARNING MENU

On the basis of what you know about your class members, their needs and the ways in which they learn best, choose at least one learning activity from each of the three Dimensions.

To facilitate your planning, take time before the first class session to read this entire leader's guide. Some activities call for collection of supplies before the session. Some suggest writing for additional information. Time spent in planning now will shorten planning and worry time later on.

Opening Prayer
Almighty and ever-living God,
ruler of all things in heaven and earth,
hear our prayers . . .
Strengthen the faithful,
arouse the careless,
and restore the penitent.
Grant us all things necessary for our common life,
and bring us all to be of one heart and mind
within your holy church;
through Jesus Christ our Lord. Amen.

(From *Book of Common Worship*, © 1993 Westminster/John Knox Press; page 803. Used by permission of Westminster/John Knox Press.)

Dimension 1: What Does the Bible Say?

(A) Tour the city of Rome.

Before the session:
- Hang a map showing Paul's world on the classroom wall. (An excellent map can be found in the *Bible Teacher Kit*, Abingdon, 1994.)
- Locate the *Bible Teacher Kit*.
- Prepare the television monitor and VCR hookups.
- If desired, invite guests who have traveled in Rome.
- Secure brochures on modern Rome from a local travel agency.

When the activity begins:
- Ask class members to locate Rome on the wall map or the map in the study book (inside cover). Using the Scale of Miles, ask them to estimate the distance from Jerusalem to Rome. Note that Paul's trip to Rome was either by boat on often perilous waterways or by walking the dusty roads.
- Show the video of Bible lands found in the *Bible Teacher Kit*. Use only the section "Places Paul Visited" (approximately 15 minutes in length). This will orient the class to the geographical settings for sessions of this unit: Rome,

Corinth, Ephesus, Galatia, and Philippi. Or you may choose to show only the segment of the video that describes Rome (approximately 4 minutes in length).
- Class members or other persons in your community who have traveled in Europe and have visited Rome may be invited to share their experiences, and their color slides!
- Display brochures that tell about the modern city of Rome.

(B) Answer Dimension 1 questions.

TEACHING TIP
Class discussion will be enhanced if, before coming to class, students have read the session 1 material and have searched in the Bible for answers to the questions in Dimension 1. As class members arrive, encourage them either to review their answers or to begin the Bible search now. Save most of the class time for Dimensions 2 and 3.

Invite students who have not already done so to write out their answers to the questions in their study books. Answers to Dimension 1 questions include the following:

1. In 3:21-24 Paul described as a "gift" the righteousness of God for all who believe in Jesus Christ. It is important to note these things: this gift does not depend upon obedience to the law; the sole requirement is faith in Jesus Christ; and "gift" is a result of God's grace.

2. In 4:10 Paul discussed the relationship between Abraham's faith and his circumcision. First, Abraham received God's righteousness through faith; then, as a sign of this righteousness already given, he received circumcision. Through this sequence Paul sought to show that faith is possible without circumcision. Paul also underscored his conviction that those who are circumcised are called to follow the faith of Abraham before his circumcision.

3. The law brings wrath (4:15). God's wrath is not an angry and vengeful wrath directed to humanity, but a wrath that is directed to the forces of evil.

4. In 4:13 Paul wrote that God's promise to Abraham was that he and his descendants would inherit the world. See activity (C).

(C) Find God's promises to Abraham and Sarah.

Before the session:
- While students are encouraged to bring Bibles to each class session, provide additional copies. Provide chalkboard, chalk and erasers, or a large sheet of paper and markers.

When the activity begins:
- Recall when Paul mentioned God's promise that Abraham and his descendants would inherit the world, he was referring to the promises as found in Genesis 17:4-8, 15-19.
- Divide the class into groups of two to four persons.

- Ask half of the groups to read Genesis 17:4-8 and to list God's promises to Abraham.
- Ask the other half to read Genesis 17:15-19 and to list God's promises to Sarah. (Remind the group that Paul did not include Sarah as one of the recipients of God's promises!)
- As groups report, list the findings on chalkboard or a large sheet of paper. Items noted will include the following: Abraham and Sarah would be given many descendants; they would be the father and mother of many nations; they would have a son whom they should name Isaac; some of their descendants would be kings; God would be God to Abraham's descendants forever; Abraham and his descendants would possess the land of Canaan forever.

Dimension 2: What Does the Bible Mean?

(D) How many ways can you say "righteousness of God"?

Before the session:
- Provide a variety of translations of the New Testament.

When the activity begins:
- Distribute Bibles to selected class members, asking each to find Romans 1:16-17. Ask readers to report, indicating the translation they read and the reading that translation gives for the term "the righteousness of God." (For example: The New English Bible translates the righteousness of God as "God's way of righting wrong"; The New Testament in Modern English, "God's plan for imparting righteousness to men"; The Bible: An American Translation, "God's way of uprightness"; Good News for Modern Man, "How God puts men right with himself.")
- On chalkboard or a large sheet of paper, draw two columns. Label the first column "Righteousness." Ask the class to list as many synonyms for this word as is possible in two minutes.
- Note that the study book indicates that Paul's Greek might better be translated "justice" than "righteousness." Label a second column "justice" and repeat the exercise.
- Suggest that class members read 1:16-17 in unison, replacing *righteousness* with *justice* and *righteous* with *just*.
- Discuss the question:
—In what way, if any, does this reading feel different from the NRSV and other versions read in class?

(E) Relate God's grace and "saying grace."

- Consider:
—What is the relationship between "the grace of God" and "saying grace" before meals? (God's grace requires a grateful response.)

- Encourage members to share some traditional family mealtime prayers or "graces." (If they are not readily recalled, suggest that they bring them next week when they can be shared at the beginning of the session, or posted on the class bulletin board.)

> **Nineteenth Century Table Grace**
> Our Father in heaven, we thank thee for this another manifestation of thy loving kindness toward us. Pardon all our sins and imperfections; and lead us by thy Spirit through our pathway of life. Bless this food to its intended use and us to thy service; and finally in heaven save us, we ask it for Christ's sake. Amen.
> (Urias Feller, Portage County, Indiana)

- Read the "Nineteenth Century Table Grace" aloud. Ask:
— What God-given gifts are specifically mentioned or implied?
— For what other life experiences might we say "grace"?
- Ask the group to choose one of these life experiences for which they will write a "grace." You may want to do this exercise as a class or divide into smaller writing teams (particularly if your class is large). Provide large sheets of paper, markers, and masking tape.

(F) Debate: believing or doing.

Paul suggested that Abraham was rewarded because he believed God, not because he succeeded in doing works of the law.
- Discuss the questions:
— Can believing and doing be separated?
— Is one more important than the other?
— Does one of them come before the other?
- Divide the class into two groups. Assign one as the "doing" group and one as the "believing" group.
- Let each group choose one member to represent it in a debate. The group's responsibility is to supply its representative with as many reasons as possible to support the premise that either doing or believing is most important. (If the class is large it may be divided into four or six groups with each group choosing a spokesperson.)
- Allow five minutes for these groupings. Reassemble the groups.
- Allow two minutes for each spokesperson to state his or her case, and one minute for each to give a rebuttal. Allow sufficient time for all members to engage in general discussion.
- Review questions in the first paragraph of this activity.
— How will class members answer them now?

Dimension 3: What Does the Bible Mean to Us?

(G) Write a letter to the church, in the style of Paul.

Before the session:
- Provide an 8 1/2-by-11-inch paper for each class member with the following paraphrase of Romans 1:1-7 at the top of the page:
— I, a servant of Jesus Christ, called to be an apostle, set apart for the gospel of God . . .
— . . . including yourselves who are called to belong to Jesus Christ,
— to all God's beloved in _____, (write name of your town in the space provided)
— who are called to be saints:
— Grace to you and peace from God our Father and the Lord Jesus Christ.

When the activity begins:
- Provide pencils for those who need them.
- Ask persons to complete this letter by writing their own personal messages to the church today.
- Carefully observe this process. As people seem to finish, group them together to share with each other, allowing others to continue with their writing.
- Call the group together. Ask these questions:
— How did it feel to write a letter to the church?
— Did you write to a particular church, to a particular denomination, or to the entire Christian church?
— Can you summarize in one sentence your message to the church?

(H) Find evidence of trying to be like God.

Before the session:
- Provide the following materials: copies of newspapers from the week just ended; enough scissors for each person; paste, glue, or transparent tape; and a long strip of newsprint or butcher paper at least six feet long, mounted horizontally on the wall, and titled "WE TRIED TO BE LIKE GOD."

When the activity begins:
- Remind the class of the material in the study book (page 6) that described sin not as *failing* to be "like God" but as *trying* to be like God.
- Ask class members to find and cut out newspaper items that illustrate humanity's tendency to try to be like God. (Items describing the failure to be like God would probably be easier to find.)

- Direct that the items be mounted on the large piece of paper.
- Share the content of items discovered, discussing how they fit the title of the display. Affirm efforts of the group and acknowledge that this may have been a difficult activity since one common concept of sin is falling short of being God-like. (Sin as trying to be like God may be a completely new idea.)

(I) Discover our common heritage: life.

Before the session:
- Set up an opaque projector.
- Photocopy Romans 3:21-24 so that class members can read the passage in unison at the end of the activity. If you do not have access to a photocopier, provide copies of the same Bible translation.

When the activity begins:
- Share: Regardless of our diversity, all humanity shares one common characteristic—the Creator's gift of life!

- Project onto a screen or a light-colored wall the Family Circus cartoon.
- After a moment of enjoying the cartoonist's insight, ask class members to share a word or two that describes one of life's gifts. (Be aware that some gifts mentioned may not be reality for all people—those with physical limitations, the socially oppressed, or the poor, for example. Keep pressing for life's gifts available to all persons.)
- Conclude by reading in unison Romans 3:21-24.

(J) Speculate: why Abraham?

A question is raised by the author of the study book (page 10). No right answer is given! "It is worth pondering the apostle's choice of Abraham as his example of faith. Why Abraham and not Jesus? And if Abraham, why not Sarah, too?"
- Invite half of the class members to discuss the reasons why Paul should have used Jesus as an example of faith and why this might not have been appropriate.
- Invite the other half of the class to discuss the reasons Paul should have chosen Sarah as an example of faith and why this might not have been appropriate.
- Discuss conclusions as a total group. Ask someone to try to summarize the results of this activity.
- Ask: If Paul were writing a letter today, who might he cite as persons of faith?

(K) Consider the impartiality of God.

The study book suggests that one affirmation of this focus passage is the concept that before God, all human beings are equal (page 3). Romans 2:11 states it succinctly: "For God shows no partiality." While God may see all humanity as equal, human beings do not see each other this way!
- Invite class members to think silently about this question for two minutes:
—Who are the "unequal" in this community?
- Continue the silence as members ponder another question:
—What should be the role of the church, if any, in changing the way we as human beings view each other?
- Break the silence. Invite class members to share feelings, insights, or suggestions. (Do not insist upon verbal response at this time. Some classes may be ready to engage in animated discussion. Some may want to launch a plan of action that will save the world! Others will need to ponder in their hearts.)

(L) Listen to humanity's "fall" in music.

Before the session:
- Secure from a library or personal collection a recording of Handel's *Messiah*.
- Set up audio equipment (record, CD, or tape player).

When the activity begins:
- Share: In Romans 5:12-21 Paul places in juxtaposition the sin of Adam in the Garden of Eden and the grace of God in Christ Jesus. Handel picks up this theme in the *Messiah* chorus that contains the lines "as in Adam all die, even so in Christ shall all be made alive."
- Invite a class member to read aloud Romans 5:12-17.
- Play the chorus that contains the lines "as in Adam all die" and follow it with a playing of the "Hallelujah!" chorus. Encourage people to talk about this music, their former experiences of hearing or singing the music of the *Messiah*, and the meaning it has for them.

(M) Write it down.

Suggest that each person purchase an inexpensive spiral notebook. As soon after class as possible, suggest that each class member record in it any new insights they have discovered in this class session and any questions that have emerged that are not yet resolved. This will be a private notebook, added to after each session.

Additional Bible Helps

Who Wrote the Letter?

Who wrote this letter? Among scholars of the New Testament there is no question about the writer of the Letter to the Romans; Paul wrote it. The only question is whether it was originally in the form in which we have it today. There is some evidence that a shortened version of the letter was in early circulation, consisting only of Romans 1–14, plus the closing benediction in 16:25-27.

There is also speculation that chapter 16 may have been a separate letter, perhaps to the church at Ephesus, rather than the church at Rome.

What Was the Purpose of the Letter?

Earlier tradition assumed that this letter, as perhaps the last of Paul's writings, was a summary of his theological thought. This now seems unlikely since theological issues included in other letters do not appear in Romans, namely baptism and the Lord's Supper. If not a systematic theology, then for what purpose did he write it?

It has been suggested that Paul was seeking support for his expanding missionary efforts among Gentiles, as well as authentication from Jewish Christians of Jerusalem. If he could secure financial support from Roman Christians, he would be able to provide money for Jerusalem Christians who had been experiencing famine, and thus authenticate with them his ministry among the Gentiles. Furthermore, in anticipation of his planned trip to Spain (Romans 15:22-29), Paul needed monetary support that he hoped to receive from the church in Rome. So for whatever reasons, this letter served to officially introduce him to the Christians in Rome prior to his planned visit.

On the other hand, if not intended as a systematic presentation of his theology, perhaps this letter, like the others, was pastoral in nature. About A.D. 49 Claudius, the emperor of Rome, expelled all of the Jews from Rome. Some ancient writers attributed this action to a disturbance caused by "Chrestus" (Christos). The nature of the disturbance is unclear, but it may have been a problem within the Jewish community because the Jewish Christians were proclaiming Jesus as the Christ. At the death of Claudius in A.D. 54 the expelled Jews returned to Rome. Now the conflict may have been within the Christian community itself over issues of seniority. In the intervening years new leadership must have emerged to replace those who had been expelled. Upon the return of expelled leaders, what then would be their role? Rather than centering on Paul's missionary activities and the needs of Jerusalem Christians, the purpose of the letter may have been to address conflicts within the church at Rome.

While some of this is speculation, it is speculation based on an informed knowledge of historical events, and an understanding of Paul and his missionary activity.

The probability is that rather than one purpose, Paul's letter to Rome was in response to a mosaic of circumstances.

The Roman Empire: A Dominant Force

All the events of the New Testament are set within a time dominated by the authority of the Roman Empire. Jesus began his life in Bethlehem because his family traveled there to comply with Roman census requirements; he ended his life at the order of a Roman governor. While the cross was an ancient invention, its use had been standardized and ritualized by Rome.

Paul was a Roman citizen and served his entire ministry within the bounds of the Roman Empire. His longest letter was to the church at Rome. His ministry finally came to an end at the hands of Roman powers. Ironically, it was his arrest by Romans at Jerusalem that made it possible for him finally to reach Rome. Here he made his appeal to Caesar, as was his right as a Roman citizen.

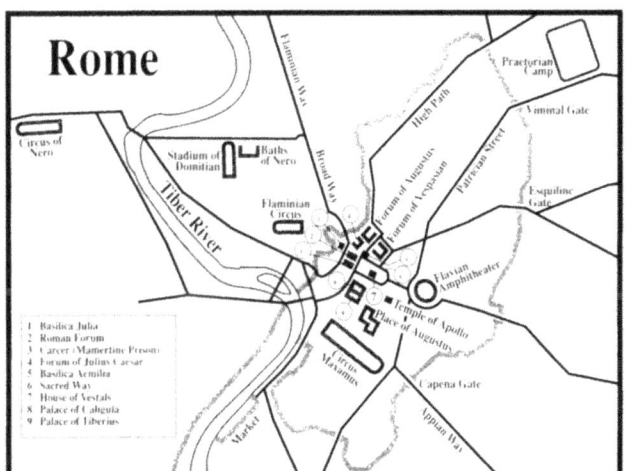

The City of Rome

Rome was the major city of the Roman Empire. When Paul visited Rome, it was already a city of over one million people. It was set on seven hills and surrounded by a wall over thirteen miles in circumference. Public buildings and homes of the rich were magnificent in size and appearance. A system of lead pipes connected these buildings to the sewage system. Most citizens, however, were crowded together in wooden or brick tenements, sometimes six stories high. These dwellings had no heat, water, or latrines. They were in constant danger of fire, and burned rapidly in the fire of A.D. 64 when Nero was emperor.

2 Romans 8:18-39
A Vision of Freedom

LEARNING MENU

Based on what you know about your class members, their needs and the ways in which they learn best, choose at least one learning activity from each of the three Dimensions.

Opening Prayer

Eternal God,
you sent us a Savior, Christ Jesus,
to break down the walls of hostility that divide us.
Send peace on earth,
and put down greed, pride, and anger,
which turn nation against nation and race against race.
Speed the day when wars will end
and the whole world accepts your rule;
through Jesus Christ our Lord. Amen.

(From *Book of Common Worship*, © 1993 Westminster/John Knox Press; page 100. Used by permission of Westminster/John Knox Press.)

Dimension 1: What Does the Bible Say?

(A) Answer Dimension 1 questions.

● Ask class members to share answers they have found. Through brief discussion clarify what the Bible says.

1. The two intercessors identified in this passage are the Spirit (Romans 8:27) and Christ Jesus who died and was raised from the dead (8:34).

2. Creation waits with eager longing for the "revealing of the children of God" (8:19) and hopes to be delivered from bondage and decay (8:21).

3. Humanity waits for adoption, the redemption of our bodies (8:23).

4. What has God done? God searches the heart (27); God predestines to be conformed to the Son's image (29); God calls (30); God justifies (30, 33); God glorifies (30); God gave up the Son for all of us (32); God loves [us] (39).

TEACHING TIP

Continue to encourage class members to read the biblical materials ahead of time and to write answers to questions in the study book. Provide a limited amount of time for this at the beginning of the session. Use most of the class time for Dimensions 2 and 3.

(B) Share key verses.

- Invite class members to silently skim this focus passage (Romans 8:18-39), finding any verse that leaps out as especially meaningful for them.
- As they are willing, ask members to read aloud the verse selected. (If the class is a large class, let people share in groups of six to ten.)
- Conclude with a unison reading of verses 38 and 39.

Dimension 2:
What Does the Bible Mean?

(C) Study a hymn.

Before the session:
- Gather enough copies of your church's hymnals so that each class member will have a copy to use during this session.
- Secure a few extra Bibles in case class members have forgotten to bring theirs.

When the activity begins:
- Share: "Our study book asserts that the concept of the Trinity is not a Pauline doctrine. In fact, fourteen hymn texts in one denominational hymnal are listed under the subject of Trinity, but only one of these is footnoted to a Bible text. And this text is not directed to the relationship between God, Holy Spirit and Christ." Ask the class to do its own study.
- Help class members locate in the hymnal the subject index and the specific subject, "Trinity."
- As members call out the hymn numbers found under this subject heading, write them on the chalkboard or a large sheet of paper. Draw lines to divide this list into four groups.
- Ask the class to number off by four. Persons who are number "1" will locate hymns in group "1," and so forth.
- Instruct the groups to locate the hymn, then direct its attention to the footnote in order to discover the biblical basis for this hymn. If a biblical reference is found, the group should locate it in the Bible and discover if it is a reference to "Trinity" or to some other subject.
- Begin with the first hymn listed on chalkboard or paper; ask class members to report their findings.
- Summarize:
—What basis in Scripture have hymn writers found for the concept of "Trinity"?

(D) Ponder "a time for patient waiting."

Sonnet on His Blindness

When I consider how my light is spent
Ere half my days in this dark world and wide,
And that one Talent which is death to hide,
Lodged with me useless, though my Soul more bent
To serve therewith my Maker, and present
My true account, lest He returning chide,
"Doth God exact day-labour, light denied,"
I fondly ask. But Patience, to prevent
That murmur, soon replies, "God doth not need
Either man's work or his own gifts.
Who best
Bear his mild yoke, they serve him best.
His state
Is kingly: thousands at his bidding speed,
And post o're land and ocean without rest;
They also serve who only stand and wait."

—Milton, 1655

- Share: Modern life is more oriented to action than to waiting; yet the study book reminds us that for Paul the present "is a time for patient waiting" (page 15). Faced with loss of eyesight at the relatively early age of forty-two, John Milton penned a sonnet on his blindness.
- Read the poem aloud.
- Ask class members to listen for the feelings expressed by the poet.
- Invite class members to describe these feelings in two or three words.
—How do they respond to the last line of the poem?
- Read aloud the last paragraph of the study book for this session.
- Discuss:
—How does one take responsibility while waiting?
—What would be the content of a prayer prayed by someone who is "serving" by "waiting"?
- Help the group create such a prayer, or ask each member individually to write "A Prayer to Be Prayed While Waiting" that they will use in their personal devotional life.

Waiting

"Our time is a time of waiting; waiting is its special destiny.... waiting for the breaking in of eternity .... All time, both in history and in personal life, is expectation. Time itself is waiting, waiting not for another time, but for that which is eternal" (*The Shaking of the Foundations*, by Paul Tillich; Charles Scribner's Sons, 1948; page 152).

(E) Discover what we already know.

- Before the session, prepare for each class member a "cinquain" worksheet (see box).

- Say: "Inside of each of us are things we *know* but have never *learned* and that we do not know we know! Writing a cinquain poem, a poetry form from France, is one way to discover insights we may have never explored."

- Give each person a worksheet that looks like this:

CINQUAIN

Title, noun, (one word)

Describe title (two words)

Action words or a phrase (three words)

Feeling words about title (four words)

Word that means same as title (one word)

Here is a sample cinquain about joy.

Joy
Emotion, Feeling
Laughing, Smiling, Clapping
Cheerful, Glad, Lighthearted, Exultant
Happiness

- Ask persons on the right side of the room to insert as the title of their poem, "HOPE" and on left side of the room, "GLORY."
- Allow several minutes for each to complete the poem.
- Encourage persons to share their poems with the whole group.
- Hear the "HOPE" poems first. Ask members to recall key words they heard and write these on chalkboard or a large sheet of paper.
- Hear "GLORY" poems next, following the same procedure.
- Remind students of the sentence in their study book: "The hope of which Paul writes is the hope of sharing God's glory." Ask:
—What new insights do you now have about this sentence?

(F) Define *freedom*.

- Before the session, provide a dictionary and a thesaurus.

When the activity begins:

- Share: "Our nation has been called a 'land of freedom.' Teenagers insist that freedom is their right. Each of us, in our own way, longs for the quality of life that freedom can bring."
- Ask someone to read the definition of *freedom* from a dictionary.
- Read to the class the variety of synonyms for *freedom* found in a thesaurus.
- Discuss:
—The title of this session is "A Vision of Freedom." When Paul spoke of freedom, what was his vision?

Dimension 3: What Does the Bible Mean to Us?

(G) Discover new meanings for ourselves.

TEACHING TIP
This option may be done in tandem with option (H) or it may stand alone.

- Share: Freedom from sin and freedom for new life are goals with which few Christians would quarrel. But what contemporary people want to know is *What does this mean in my life today?*
- Divide a chalkboard into three columns, or provide for three large pieces of paper.
- Title the first column "FOR" and ask the questions:
—Why do we want freedom?
—If we really had freedom, what could we have that we do not have now?
- Accept and record the responses without comment.
- Title the second column "FROM" and ask the question:
—In order to secure the values in column one, from what do we need to free ourselves? List these as before.
- Finally, title the third column "PRICE" and ask:
—In order to achieve the quality of life we desire, what will it cost us?
- Record responses.
- Discuss:
—Are the values we desire worth the price?

(H) Find new meanings for our nation.

If you chose to lead your class in option (G) the responses may have been in terms of one's personal life. This option follows the same sequence found in option (G) but changes the questions.

- Ask:
—Why do we want freedom for our nation?
—From what does our nation need to free itself?

—In order to achieve the values we desire for our nation, what will it cost us personally, and what will it cost us as a nation?
—Are the values worth the price?

(I) Find new meanings for our church.

Follow the same sequence as in options (G) and (H) but for the word *nation* in the questions, substitute the words *our church*. Answering these questions may be more difficult than (G) or (H)!

(J) Find a way to say "I'm sorry."

Before the session:
- Fold pieces of typing paper into quarters to simulate a greeting card.
- Provide two blank "cards" for each person you expect to be present.
- Place cards, pencils, and markers on tables.

When the activity begins:
- Share: "Personal suffering and national agonies exist but for Paul these were not attributed to "God's will." Nevertheless, to say "It is God's will" is a common response with which people sometimes seek to console those who have suffered a loss.
- Suggest that class members make two sympathy cards: one they consider "typical" and one with a meaningful message they think they would like to receive when they experience a loss.
- When most class members have completed this task, gather them together to discuss this question:
—What are your ideas for an ideal sentiment to appear on a sympathy card?
—What message might Paul put in such a card?

TEACHING TIP
Churches often sell Christmas cards. Maybe your class would like to design a sympathy card for sale to church members.

(K) Sing a hymn.

God's gift of the created universe is for people of all ages and places and is celebrated in song in many languages.
- Find these hymns: "All Things Bright and Beautiful", a traditional children's hymn (*The United Methodist Hymnal*, No. 147); "Many and Great, O God," set to a Native American melody (No. 148); and "God Created Heaven and Earth," a traditional Taiwanese hymn (No. 151). Finally find the hymn "Cantemos al Senor" (No. 149).
- Even if your class does not know Spanish, encourage them to try the Spanish before turning to the English words.

Sources for Information on Environmental Issues

- Telephone book. For local sources see "Environmental, Conservation, and Ecological Organizations" in the classified Yellow Pages;
- Local library. Consult card catalogue;
- Citizens Clearing House for Hazardous Waste. P.O. Box 6806, Falls Church, VA 22040;
- Friends of the Earth. 218 D Street S.E., Washington, DC 20003;
- Greenpeace. 1436 U Street, NW, Washington, DC, 20009; 202-462-1177. An international organization dedicated to preserving the earth and all the life it supports. There are regional offices in Chicago, San Francisco, Seattle, and New York. Greenpeace stores are in Provincetown, MA; Key West, FL; and San Francisco, CA;
- National Wildlife Federation. 1400 16th St. N.W., Washington, DC 20036;
- Peace Resource Project. P.O. Box 1122, Arcata, CA, 95521; 1-800-829-6202;
- Rainforest Action Network. 301 Broadway Street, #A, San Francisco, CA 94133;
- Sierra Club. 730 Polk Street, San Francisco, CA 94109. An organization to help people convert concern about the health of the planet into effective environmental action. There are local chapters in every state and the District of Columbia. To locate yours contact Sierra Club Volunteer Development at the above address, 415/923-5576.

(L) Discover your church's EQ (Environmental Quotient).

Helping to preserve God's gift of creation can begin with God's people, with each church community. This activity has two parts.
Part I: Discover ways in which your church can be a more responsible inhabitant of this planet. Begin this process during this session.
Part II: Plan how you can offer the time and leadership skills of your class to help make this possible. Develop a task force from your class to initiate a plan or to work with environmental projects already underway in your church.
- Invite to your class persons in your church responsible for church property maintenance. Include at least one member of the board of trustees and the church custodian. Assure them in advance that this is a "fact-finding" activity, not a "fault-finding" or "blame-assessing" exercise.
- Begin with general, open-ended questions:
—Has the church had an energy audit done by local utilities?

- —If so, what changes have been made as a result of the audit?
- —Does the church have an environmental protection policy in place? If so, what does it include?
- Move to more specific questions:
- —What method is used for disposal of food scraps, grass clippings, and other organic materials?
- —Could these be composted for use in church flower beds and vegetable gardens?
- —Could excess compost be made available to church members for use in their yards?
- —Is energy-efficient refrigeration used in the church kitchen?
- —If not, would trustees consider this an option when present refrigerators need to be replaced?
- —How much of the kitchen garbage consists of paper and plastic products such as paper or plastic cups and plates, paper table cloths, paper napkins, and so forth.
- —How can this amount be reduced?
- —Is there a plan for recycling glass, cans, and plastic containers?
- —Is there a recycle bin beside the soft drink machine?
- —What kind of detergent is used for dishwashing, cleaning, and laundry?
- —If it is not phosphate-free, would this be an option?
- —Has the heating system been inspected recently with respect to preventing heat loss?
- —Are water heaters and furnaces well insulated?
- —Are heating zones regulated by thermostats so that unused rooms during the week are not heated?
- —Are windows and doors weatherstripped to prevent heat loss?
- —Are energy-saving light bulbs being used where appropriate?
- —Do timers automatically turn lights off at hours when not needed?
- —What kind of paper is purchased for church office use?
- —Could the use of recycled paper be established as a priority?
- —Is there a box in the church office where paper appropriate for recycling can be placed?
- —How does the church try to conserve water?
- —Are there low-flow attachments on faucets?
- —Are there displacement devices such as sealed and water-filled plastic bottles in toilet tanks?
- —Can sprinklers and hoses be adjusted so that water goes on the grass and not on concrete sidewalks and driveways? (Assume that dripping faucets are repaired promptly!)
- At this point in the session the work yet to be done may seem overwhelming! Remember, Rome wasn't built in a day! Ask for volunteers for a small task force to summarize the findings of this session and bring a proposal later for further action.

(M) Sell a bumper sticker.

- Plan to sponsor the sale of "Think Globally—Act Locally" bumper stickers. Set a goal that every car bumper in your church will have either this one or one with a similar message.
- Plan an "Environmental Booth" for your church's next bazaar, and sell the bumper stickers there. (For quantity prices call Peace Resource Project. See the box on sources for information on environmental issues.)

(N) Write it down.

- Remind members to write new insights and unresolved questions in their notebooks as soon as it is convenient.

Additional Bible Helps

The "For Us-Ness" of God

The Bible clearly affirms that God is for us. Throughout the succession of events recorded in the Bible, God plainly shows active concern for all persons. This concern takes many forms but shows itself primarily in the ways God acts. God punishes, approves, shows mercy, loves. God has high hopes for us and confidence in us. God is for us and against anything that diminishes us. Even when we really foul things up, the reality of God's "for us-ness" holds out to us the possibility of new life.

The Most Dramatic Evidence

Jesus Christ is the most dramatic evidence of God's "for us-ness." He is both the messenger and the message. It is as if God has pulled out all the stops at once in an effort to convince us of our own worthiness. (From *Experiencing the Bible With Children*, by Dorothy Jean Furnish, Abingdon, 1990; pages 36-37)

Glory

The Hebrew word *kabod* (translated "glory") means "weight" or "importance." Thus, to talk of God's glory is to acknowledge the importance of God.

The term *glory* is used throughout both the Old Testament and New Testament. It is often used to characterize God, and/or God's presence. Sometimes it is used to describe humans; and in the New Testament it is used to describe both God and the risen Christ. When used in terms of the end of time, it is associated with Christ's return when humanity will participate in God's glory.

Even though the hope of Paul may at times seem to center on the end of the age, it is important to note the assertion made in the study book: "Because the future belongs to God, so does the present, and it is the present life on which Paul is mainly focused..." (page 15).

3

CHRISTIANS AND JEWS

Romans 11:11-36

LEARNING MENU

Based on what you know about your class members, their needs and the ways in which they learn best, choose at least one learning activity from each of the three Dimensions.

Opening Prayer

How great is your love, Lord God,
how wide is your mercy!
Never let us board up the narrow gate that leads to life
with rules or doctrines that you dismiss;
but give us a Spirit to welcome all people with
affection,
so that your church may never exclude secret friends of
yours,
who are included in the love of Jesus Christ,
who came to save us all. Amen.

(From *Book of Common Worship*, © 1993 Westminster/John Knox Press, 1993; page 804 used by permission of Westminster/John Knox Press.)

Dimension 1: What Does the Bible Say?

(A) Answer Dimension 1 questions.

Answers to the questions in the study book include the following:

1. In Romans 11:17-24 Paul was speaking to the Gentiles as the "branches" that have been grafted onto the roots of the olive tree (the historic Israel). The Jews who have rejected the gospel are "the natural branches," which have been cut off.

2. In 11:25-36 Paul named as "mystery" the fact that part of Israel had rejected the gospel. He called it a "hardening" that had come upon Israel (25).

3. In 11:29 the gifts and the calling of God are described as "irrevocable"; they cannot be retracted or revoked.

4. In 11:30-32 readers are assured that even for those who are disobedient to God, God's mercy is extended to all.

(B) Compare "dough" and "olive trees."

- Share the following information: In Romans 11:11-16 Paul mixed his metaphors, speaking of "dough" and "roots" in the same breath. His Gentile Roman readers may have been as confused as readers in twentieth century United States!
- Ask class members to compare Numbers 15:17-21 and Romans 11:16. In the light of Numbers, what did Paul seem to be saying in Romans 11:16? (The first batch of dough is made into a loaf and given to God as a symbol that the whole batch is holy—that it is all from God. Similarly, if the roots of the olive tree represent historic Israel, then its branches, whether Jew or Gentile, are also of God.)

(C) Feel Paul's distress.

- Share the following information: The study book suggests that in Romans 9:1-5 Paul was expressing his concern that "his own people" had been unreceptive to the gospel of Christ.
- Invite class members to form groups of two. Their task is threefold:
—Read the passage silently, or one partner may read aloud;
—Talk about how Paul must have felt;
—Rewrite the passage, using terminology a modern Paul might use.
- Ask partners to share their work with the class as they are willing.

Dimension 2: What Does the Bible Mean?

(D) Research topics.

Three of the ideas in this focus passage can be prepared by research groups and presented to the entire class for clarification and discussion.

- Divide the class into three sections. Each section will prepare a report on its understanding of the topic assigned to it and will choose one member to share this with the class.
—Section 1 Topic: "Conversion versus Call." Read Romans 1:1-7 and the paragraph on page 21 of the study book that begins, "What we often think of as Paul's 'conversion'..."
—Section 2 Topic: "Unconditional Faithfulness of God." Read Romans 10:21 and the paragraph in the study book on page 22 that begins, "A fundamental and recurring theme..."
—Section 3 Topic: "God's Plan." Read Romans 11:11-12 and the paragraph in the study book on page 22 that begins, "After acknowledging that..." (Since this is a complex concept, this group may need the leader's help. However, before you join them, let the group struggle with their task for a few minutes.)
- After each group has reported to the class, allow time for clarification and discussion.

(E) Study a hymn.

Before the session:
- Arrange for an instrumental accompanist for a hymn.
- Locate the hymn "There's a Wideness in God's Mercy." (Many denominational hymnals include this hymn, which partially captures the magnitude of God's unconditional faithfulness. It is No. 121 in *The United Methodist Hymnal*.)
- Hang an eight-foot strip of butcher paper divided into four columns, or four large pieces of paper, on which class members can write or draw. At the top of the first column print the first stanza of the hymn; at the top of the second column, stanza 2, and so on to include all four stanzas. (See the sidebar, "There's a Wideness in God's Mercy.")
- Provide markers of various colors.

"There's a Wideness in God's Mercy"

(1) There's a wideness in God's mercy like the wideness of the sea; there's a kindness in God's justice, which is more than liberty.

(2) There is welcome for the sinner, and more graces for the good! There is mercy with the Savior; there is healing in his blood.

(3) For the love of God is broader than the measure of our mind; and the heart of the Eternal is most wonderfully kind.

(4) If our love were but more simple, we should rest upon God's word; and our lives would be illumined by the presence of our Lord.

When the activity begins:
- Divide the class into four groups.
- Assign to each group one of the stanzas of the hymn.
- Ask each group to imagine that they are photographers, seeking to take a color slide that will illustrate their assigned stanza.
- Suggest that they first describe the picture in words.
- As groups finish instruct them to write their description in the appropriate column. Encourage them to actually sketch the picture they are describing with colored markers provided.
- Let each group share its contribution and something of the conversation that accompanied the process.

- Finally, gather the class around the mural and sing the hymn!
  (This would be an appropriate activity with which to end the session.)

(F) Create a banner.

Most adult classrooms can use at least one banner displayed for a time and then replaced with another. While this project might be planned as the only activity of the session, it would be preferable to extend it over several sessions as an activity for the early part of the class.
Before the session:
- During the week before this activity is to begin, recruit two or three class members to help in selecting a phrase for the banner. It might be a phrase from the study book, such as "God's saving purpose is for all" or "God is impartial" or it might be a phrase from this session's focus passage from Romans.
- Provide materials for making the banner. (See the sidebar, "Banner Making.")

Banner Making

Banners can be simple or complicated. If this is your first banner, keep it simple! Search in your congregation for someone who is an experienced banner maker, and ask for their guidance. You will need the following:
—Materials for the background, cut to whatever size you wish your banner to be. Most people use felt, burlap, or muslin. Bright colors can be used, although you may choose a more neutral color and save bright colors for the design.
—Paper on which to draw patterns for designs.
—Multicolored cloth or felt with which to create the design.
—White or fabric glue for affixing the design pieces.
—Scissors for cutting the design pieces.
—Dowel sticks, broom handle, or curtain rod for hanging the banner.
—Needle and thread for sewing a pocket for a rod.
—A fair amount of creativity and patience!

When the activity begins:
- Have banner making materials set up and ready when the first persons arrive. As others come, invite them to join the project. If you have planned other activities for this session, give members a few moments notice so that the work may be set aside.
- Remind members that there will be opportunity to continue work on the banner at the next session.

Dimension 3:
What Does the Bible Mean to Us?

(G) Think about the question *Who am I?*

Before the session, provide blank paper and pencils for each person.

When the activity begins:
- Share:

    In Romans 11:1 Paul clarified that, even though a follower of Christ, he was still a Jew. He identified himself as "an Israelite, a descendent of Abraham, a member of the tribe of Benjamin." This assertion was repeated in others of his letters. Meetings in our culture often open with a time for introductions in which the leader will say, "Let's go around the circle; give us your name and tell us something about yourself." In other words, identify yourself. For employed persons the name is usually followed by one's occupation. People sometimes respond with information about their spouse and children. In this activity individuals have an opportunity to consider their own identity in its variety of dimensions.

- Ask members to list all of the ways they might be able to answer the question *Who are you?* Assure participants that this list is not to be shared with the group. (Answers may be in terms of occupation, gender, ancestry, race, sexual orientation, family relationships, class, or many others. How many will respond with "Christian" or their denominational affiliation?)
- Invite members to number the items on the list in their order of importance. Wait until this task has been completed before going to the next step.
- Direct members to place a checkmark by the item with which they would respond in a public meeting. Wait again.
- Ask members to place an asterisk beside the item that is most important to them personally. Again wait.
- Finally, ask members to place an "X" beside the items which they are powerless to change.
- Discuss the question:
—What did you discover in the process of doing this activity that you are willing to share? (The thoughtfulness with which most people will participate illustrates the importance they attach to identity, whether they realize it or not. We share this value with Paul!)

TEACHING TIP

Identity is addressed in another way in Session 11, activities (D) and (L).

(H) View a video about the Holocaust.

Before the session:
- Secure the video. (Some possible sources: a local rabbi may be able to suggest an available video, which accurately portrays this period of history from the Jewish perspective; local public or university libraries; regional Holocaust museums; the Anti-Defamation League.)
- Be sure video equipment is set up and working.

When the activity begins:
- Share:

    As Christians we carry guilt because of our participation in the Holocaust before and during World War II. While some Christians engaged in active persecution, our overwhelming sin was one of standing by and doing nothing. (For an exception to this fact, see the sidebar, "Righteous Among the Nations.") Christians, no less than the Jewish community, should never forget this period in history.
- View the video. Provide opportunity for sharing feelings about the Holocaust.

Righteous Among the Nations

Righteous among the nations or *righteous Gentiles* is a term used to refer to those non-Jews who aided the Jews during the Holocaust. There were *righteous among the nations* in every country overrun or allied with the Nazis and their deeds often led to the rescue of Jewish lives. **Yad Vashem**, the Israeli national remembrance authority for the Holocaust bestows a special medal upon these individuals, who also are invited to plant a tree near the memorial to the martyrs of the Holocaust at **Yad Vashem**. To date, **Yad Vashem** has honored approximately 2,500 *righteous Gentiles*, after carefully evaluating each case. The country with the most righteous Gentiles, after carefully evaluating each case, is Poland. The country with the highest proportion (per population) is Holland. Moreover, this figure only includes those who actually risked their lives to save Jews and not those who merely extended aid.

[Source: "36 Questions Often Asked About the Holocaust," page 8, of a packet prepared by the University of Denver Holocaust Awareness Institute, 2040 E. Evans Ave., Suite 217, Denver, CO 80208; (303) 871-3013. Prepared in 1994 as educational materials for the fiftieth anniversary of the death of Anne Frank, celebrated in March, 1995.]

(I) Invite a survivor to share experiences.

- It is estimated that there are 350,000 survivors of the Holocaust alive today. Many of them live in the United States. Invite one living in or near your community to share experiences and insights.

(J) Discuss the study book.

- Share: The author of the study book makes this emphatic declaration: "Unquestionably, the Holocaust has forever changed the terms of the Christian-Jewish dialogue" (page 24).
- Ask class members to read in the study book Dimension 3 under "The Relationship of Christianity to Judaism," page 24, beginning, "We live in a post-Holocaust age."
- Discuss:
—What was the climate between Christians and Jews before the Holocaust?
—In what way has the Holocaust "forever changed the terms" of this climate?

(K) Identify anti-Semitism.

This may take some soul-searching. The first response may be, *There is no anti-Semitism in our town!*
- Consider:
—Is there name-calling?
—Are Jews called "Christ-killers" by "Christians"?
—Do hate signs appear when a candidate for public office is a Jew?
—Are there jokes made about Jews—their names, their customs, their idioms?
—Are Jews segregated into one area of town and abused either verbally or physically should they choose to move to another neighborhood?
—Are Jewish-owned businesses patronized or boycotted?
- Class members may say, "But there are no Jews in our community!" If true, why is this the case?
- Look at it another way:
—What is the positive evidence that anti-Semitism does not exist?
—Finally, what can this class do to begin to address anti-Semitism?

The Attitude of the Protestant Church Toward the Persecution of the Jews

The response of Protestant and Orthodox churches during the Holocaust varied. In Germany, for example, Nazi supporters within the Protestant church complied with the anti-Jewish legislation and even excluded Christians of Jewish origin from membership. Pastor Martin Niemoller's Confessing Church defended the rights of Christians of Jewish origin within the church, but did not publicly protest against their persecution, nor did it condemn the measures taken against the Jews with the exception of a memorandum it sent to Hitler in May, 1936. In occupied Europe, the stance of the Protestant churches varied. In several countries, among them Holland, France, Norway, and Denmark, local churches and/or leading clergymen issued public

> protests when the Nazis began deporting Jews. In other countries such as Yugoslavia, Bulgaria, and Greece, Orthodox church leaders intervened on behalf of the Jews and took steps which in certain cases, led to the rescue of many Jews. Non-Catholic church leaders in Austria, Belgium and Bohemia-Moravia, Finland, Italy, Poland, and Russia did not issue any public protests on behalf of the Jews.
>
> (Source: University of Denver Holocaust Awareness Institute. Used by permission.)

(L) Write it down.

- Again encourage members to record new insights discovered during this session in their notebook. See page 7, activity (M).

Additional Bible Helps

Was God's Promise Broken?
The focus passage for this session (Romans 11:11-36) is set within the context of Romans 9:1–11:36. The issue addressed in these chapters is a complex one: If the Jews are God's chosen people, has God's promise to them been broken—or at least compromised—by God's impartiality? See session 1, activity (K). How can God choose the Gentiles if the Jews are already God's chosen ones? At stake is the very nature of God—God's faithfulness to a promise. It is to this dilemma that Paul addressed the next portion of his letter to the church at Rome.

Paul began by reaffirming that the Jews are God's covenant people. He cited much of the history of the Jews, beginning with God's promise to Abraham. But Paul was perplexed at the reversal that had taken place. *How is it*, he wondered, *that the Gentiles, who did not work to achieve righteousness, have found it, while the Jews who have sought this righteousness through a disciplined and rigorous keeping of the law, have not achieved it?*

God Intentionally Reaches Out
For Paul there was no discontinuity or inconsistency between the God of Israel and the Father of Jesus Christ. God has always reached out to humankind and continues to do so, regardless of where people live or what their historical roots. Even though the Jews did not accept the gospel as a continuation of God's promise, their tradition was the basic one in which Gentile Christianity had been birthed. Paul concluded that God cannot revoke his call and his gifts and suggested (11:32) that the human inclination to disobey is intentional on God's part, so that people may experience God's mercy. Chapter 11 concludes with a majestic liturgical affirmation:

"For from him and through him and to him are all things. To him be the glory forever. Amen" (Romans 11:35).

The Relationship of Jews and Christians
The context of session 3 is Romans 9–11, a major discussion of the relationship between the Christian and Jewish communities. In addition to these three chapters, it is interesting to note other references to Jews scattered throughout Paul's letters. A reading of these references reveals several issues.

Equality Versus Uniqueness
Paul insisted that the gospel was for both Jew and Gentile, and that there is a oneness among all Christians, whether Jew or Gentile. But for Paul this affirmation did not wipe out the distinctions between these groups. He made the following observations:

- **The gospel is for the Jew first, but also for the Greek** (Gentile) (Romans 1:16; 3:29). But what does *first* mean? Does it mean that the first to affirm Jesus as Christ were the Jews? Or does it mean that Jews have some sort of prior claim to the gospel as God's chosen people?

- **Those who do evil will be punished by God**, the Jew first (Romans 2:9-10). Does this mean that because of the unique, priority status of the Jews they are judged by a more rigid standard? Or that they, more than others, must bear responsibility for their actions?

- If Jews are going to instruct others, they should instruct themselves as well. **No one is excused from accountability to God.**

- Jews have an advantage because they were trusted with the Scriptures (Romans 3:1-2).

- The bottom line for Paul, however, seems to be in 1 Corinthians 12:13: **Whether Jew or Greek, all who are baptized are filled with one spirit—the spirit of Christ.**

4

Discovering What Is Good

Romans 12:1-21

LEARNING MENU

On the basis of what you know about your class members, their needs and the ways in which they learn best, choose at least one learning activity from each of the three Dimensions.

Opening Prayer
Almighty God,
so draw our hearts to you,
so guide our minds,
so fill our imaginations,
so control our wills,
that we may be wholly yours,
utterly dedicated to you.
Use us as you will,
always to your glory and the welfare of your people;
through our Lord and Savior Jesus Christ. Amen.

(From *Book of Common Worship*, © 1993 Westminster/John Knox Press; page 829. Used by permission of Westminster/John Knox Press.)

Dimension 1: What Does the Bible Say?

(A) Answer Dimension 1 questions.

Answers to questions in the study book include the following:

1. In verse 2 Paul wrote that believers have been transformed so that they might know the will of God. The sentence structure of this verse suggests that the will of God is that which is perfect, good, and acceptable to God (1).

2. All members of Christ's body are not graced with the same gifts. In verses 6-8 these gifts are expressed in terms of functions. God gives to some the ability to prophesy, in proportion to faith; to others God gives the gifts of ministering, teaching, exhorting, giving with generosity, leading with diligence, and compassion with cheerfulness.

3. In verse 10 Paul admonished his readers to outdo one another in showing honor.

4. Believers were warned by Paul (16) not to claim more wisdom than they actually possess. This advice is reminiscent of Proverbs 3:7a, "Do not be wise in your own eyes; fear the Lord, and turn away from evil."

Dimension 2: What Does the Bible Mean?

(B) Study a hymn.

Before the session:
- Gather enough hymnals so that each participant may have one. If the hymn "Take My Life and Let It Be" (No. 399, *The United Methodist Hymnal*) is not in your congregational hymnal, write the words on a large sheet of paper or chalkboard. In at least one hymnal, this hymn is footnoted to Romans 12:1.
- Arrange for an instrumentalist to accompany the hymn.

When the activity begins:
- Form groups of three participants. Assign to each group one stanza of the hymn. (If there are more than nine persons present, more than one group can focus on a stanza.) The task is to study the verse and list the specific ways the writer of this hymn understood Paul when Paul wrote, "Present your bodies as a living sacrifice."
- Remind participants that by "bodies" Paul meant the whole, human self.
- Summarize by asking groups to report their findings. You may want to list significant information on the large sheet of paper or chalkboard, as groups report.
- Conclude this activity by again reading aloud Romans 12:1 and then leading the class in singing the hymn.

(C) Fingerpaint the "feeling" of salvation.

Before the session prepare the room for fingerpainting. Follow the suggestions in the sidebar "Preparing to Fingerpaint."

Preparing to Fingerpaint

Why? In the adult world expressing one's thoughts is often seen as more acceptable than expressing one's feelings, yet our religious life is composed of both heart and mind. Fingerpainting is one way to use the body to express feelings without having to be an artist.

How to start? The easiest way to get started, if you are unfamiliar with this teaching-learning method, is to talk with a teacher of children who has had experience with fingerpainting. You might consider inviting one to attend your class session to assist you with the mechanical aspects of this method.

What will you need? Work tables protected with a covering of newspapers; slick, white shelf paper, waxed butcher paper or fingerpaint paper; fingerpaints in several colors; spoons; water for cleaning up; paper towels; old oversized shirts, aprons, or large garbage sacks (cut holes for head and arms; "tie up" later for use as a garbage bag) as protection for clothing.

How to do it? Moisten the paper with water. Drop fingerpaint onto the paper, a spoonful at a time. Colors can be mixed if desired. Use hands (even arms) to create a design. Place paintings to dry on the floor in designated corners of the room.

- Say: "In Dimension 2 the author of the study book stresses that Paul was not telling his readers what they must do to be saved, but rather telling them that they had already been made new in Christ. This activity will help class members feel the difference between working to earn God's favor, and living with the assurance that their lives have already been made new."
- Step 1. Explain that this fingerpainting activity is also a roleplay.
- Step 2. Tell members to imagine that before they can experience God's saving power, they must earn it by their good works; the more good works, the greater assurance there will be of salvation. Then say, "Now, begin to fingerpaint, and express how you feel about this fact by your choice of colors and the flow of the paint."
- Step 3. Watch the process. It will take a few moments for participants to experiment with the paint medium. Remind them again that they will achieve salvation through their good works.
- Step 4. Ask participants to put their paintings in the designated area; all should be placed in the same corner of the room.
- Step 5. Share that the plan has been changed! Say: "The transforming power of God's love in Christ has already made your lives new. You are now called only to affirm this newness in the way you live!" Now paint how you feel!
- Step 6. Members create a second painting, placing it on the floor in a different corner of the room.
- Step 7. Encourage members to roam the room, looking at the paintings others have done, and comparing the first ones with the second ones.
- Step 8. Discuss:
—What do you notice about the paintings?
—Are there similarities?
—Is there a difference between the first and the second paintings?
—What feelings did you experience during this activity?
—Were you able to assume one of the roles more easily than the others?

(D) Answer the question: What is God's will?

- Ask class members to find in the study book the sidebar "The Will of God" on page 31. Form groups of no more than four persons. The task of each group is to read the sidebar, and then to write a one-sentence definition of "God's will." Allow about five minutes for this activity.
- Ask:
—Is God's will something in the mind of God that we are called upon to discern?
—Is it a will that God imposes onto human lives, which we are called to accept?
—Is God's will something that we are called upon to do? If so, how do we know that will for us?
- Invite each group to share its tentative definition. Emphasize that people are allowed to change their minds!
- Discuss the definitions. Suggest that members of the class be alert during the coming week for occasions when it would be appropriate to ask the question, "What is God's will?"

Dimension 3: What Does the Bible Mean to Us?

(E) Discern God's will as a community of faith.

While it is important that individuals live out their Christian faith in their personal lives, Paul also wanted the churches as communities of faith to seek to know how as the "church" they can discover what it means to act faithfully.

- Divide the class into "churches" of no more than eight to ten persons.
- Select one person in each group to be the "church leader." Hand this person a card on which you have written: "Read this card to your church: Our task for the next fifteen minutes is to plan an action project for our church. The only guidance we have is Romans 12:10-13." Give no further directions.
- Before you call the groups together for sharing, ask them to do one final task—select a name for their church.
- Ask each group to share its church name and to describe the action project it has planned.
- Discuss:
—What would it look like if this church were a "community of Christian dialogue, moral discernment, and faithful action?"
—Do any of the plans of these imaginary churches seem appropriate for our own church? If so, begin to plan how and to whom they can be presented.

(F) Discover worship in the workplace.

Before the session:
- Ask two or three members of your congregation to share with your class their experience of what it means for them to try to live out their Christian faith in their workplace. These members may or may not be in your class. Include a variety of workplaces. Be sure to include a homemaker.
- Provide markers, a large sheet of paper, and masking tape.

When the activity begins:
- As people arrive, ask each of them to draw a picture or symbols of their workplace on the large sheet of paper. After they title their work, help them post it in the room.
- Note the variety of workplaces.
- Refer the class to the paragraph on page 30 in the study book, which begins, "The offering of one's entire self to God is also described as 'spiritual worship.' " (See Romans 12:1-2.) This activity explores the meaning of spiritual worship for our life of work.
- Introduce those who have agreed to share their thoughts on faith in the workplace.

(G) Make a timeline.

To be alive is to live amid constantly changing circumstances. Over one hundred years ago the poet James Russell Lowell wrote,

> "New occasions teach new duties;
> Time makes ancient good uncouth;
> They must upward still and onward,
> Who would keep abreast of truth."

- Share: For Paul the commandment to love (Romans 13:8-10) superseded the law and was the basis for determining right action.
- Lead the class in creating a timeline showing the way love toward one's children requires different kinds of responses at different stages of their lives.
- On chalkboard or butcher paper draw a long horizontal line, divided into four sections. Label the four sections: "Infancy," "Childhood," "Adolescence," and "Young Adulthood."
- Discuss:
—What is required of parental love in each stage? The completed timeline will illustrate that changing circumstances require changed responses.
- Next ask each person to choose one of their identities. Refer to activity (G) in session 3 and make a personal timeline of changing circumstances and responses. Assure the class that the specifics of this timeline will not be shared.
- After about five minutes of individual work, ask:
—Do the personal guidelines confirm the poet's insight that "new occasions teach new duties"?

(H) Love your neighbor.

Before the session:
- Provide current newspapers (that can be cut up) and scissors.

When the activity begins:
- Say: "We live in a global village where we are all neighbors to each other." Then discuss the following question:
— How is it possible to live out Paul's admonition to love our neighbors as ourselves? (Romans 12:8-10)
- Ask some participants to cut out articles about persons who would be easy to love as neighbors.
- Ask others to cut out articles about persons who would be difficult to love as neighbors.
- Briefly share your findings.
- Discuss:
— Choose two or three newspaper or magazine clippings about "difficult neighbors." In each of these situations, what would love require?
— Was Paul being realistic?

(I) Think about our church.

- Share:
    By definition, all churches are organizations. It does not necessarily follow that all churches are communities in the sense that the members have common interests, common commitments, and are united in support of each other and these common values. It is within this kind of community of faith that we can, as community, work together to know God's will for our contemporary world. Where the total church is not a close-knit community, there are often communities within the church that serve this function.
- Ask class members to identify places in your church where they or others find supportive community.
- Next, ask if there are places outside the church where class members find such community.
- Ask:
— In what way can this group of people support and encourage community in this church?

(J) Create a class doxology.

- Share:
    The letter to the church at Rome closes with a short hymn of praise (a doxology) although it is not clear that it is from the pen of Paul. It probably indicates that the letter was read as part of worship.
- Ask members to indicate things for which this class can praise God. List things mentioned on chalkboard or newsprint.
- Choose a simple hymn tune that the class knows.
- Write a class doxology and sing it to conclude this study of the Letter to the Romans. (The doxology can be revised and polished by volunteers before next Sunday. Consider singing it each week while the class is studying Paul's letters.)

(K) Write it down.

This entry in the individual notebooks comes at the conclusion of the study of Romans. Suggest that four questions be addressed in this notebook entry:
— How do I feel about the letter to the church at Rome?
— How do I summarize what for me are the important ideas in this letter?
— What new insights have I discovered about myself and my faith journey?
— What questions do I have now for which I will continue to seek answers?

Additional Bible Helps

Paul's Reliance on the Hebrew Scriptures and Oral Tradition

Paul was an educated Jew, steeped in the writings contained in the Hebrew Scriptures. However, when he wrote his letters, probably between A.D. 50 and 60, the Gospels had not yet been written. (Mark, the first Gospel written, is placed by scholars around the year A.D. 70, approximately a dozen years later than Paul's Letter to the Romans.) What Paul did have was an oral tradition. As a follower of Jesus he must have known many of the stories and sayings that were eventually recorded in the four Gospels.

The focus passage for this session, Romans 12:1-21, is filled with verses that find some parallel in both Old Testament writings and in the Gospels. See the chart on page 22 and compare the verses from Romans with the ones from Deuteronomy, Proverbs, and Matthew. It is unlikely that the similarities could be coincidental!

Whatever Happened to Spain?

The letters Paul wrote to the churches of his founding contain a marvelous, continued story of a first century "traveling man." When last we left Paul (see session 1, "Additional Bible Helps," page 7), he was sending his letter to the church at Rome, telling them that he was on his way to Jerusalem. When he left Jerusalem, he planned to stop by Rome for a visit on his way to further missionary efforts in Spain.

In Romans 15:22-33 Paul outlined his plan to journey to Jerusalem. In effect he said, "I plan to visit you as soon as possible, but first I must go to Jerusalem to deliver to the Christians there the offering collected for them in Macedonia and Achaia. However, I make that trip to Jerusalem with some misgivings, fearing trouble from the unbelievers in Judea." Assuming Romans to be the latest of Paul's surviving letters, this is the last we hear from his own hand.

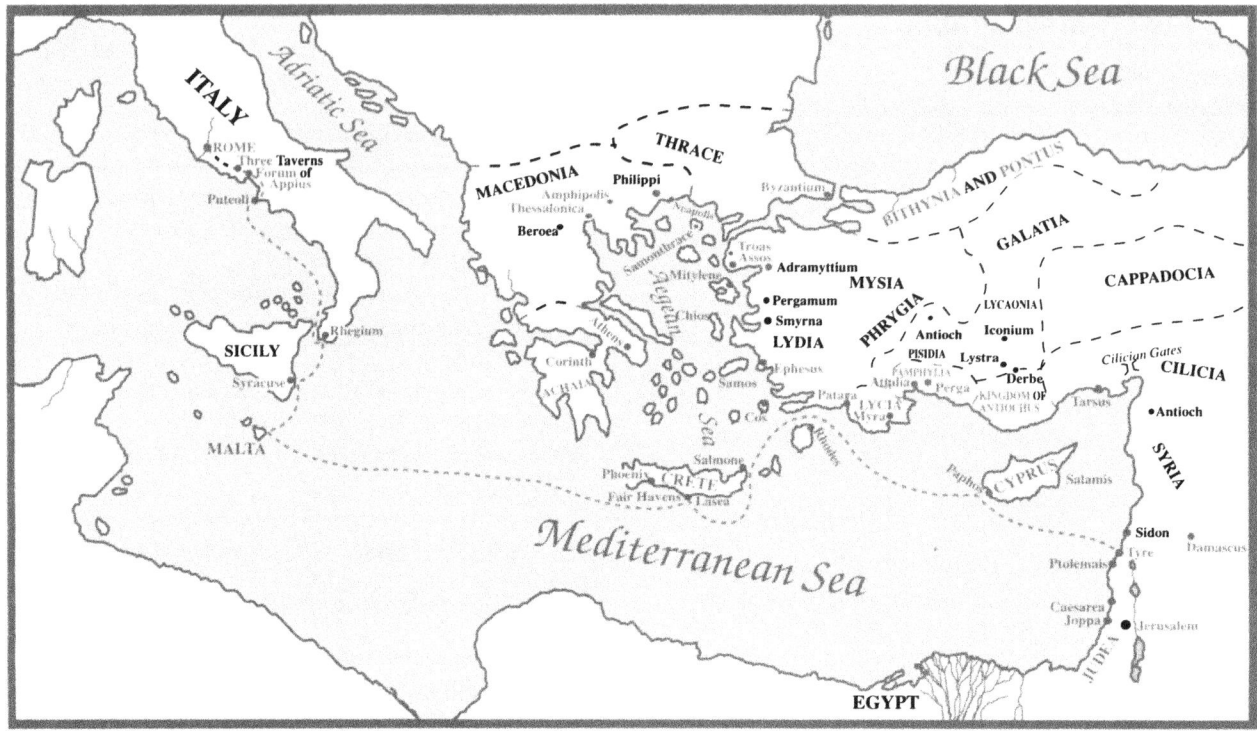

The writer of Acts, on the other hand, gives great detail about the trip to Jerusalem (Acts 20:3–21:16). A dramatic tale is recounted of Paul's arrest and trial (Acts 21:27–23:30), and his journey by sea to Rome (Acts 27:1–28:31; see the map above). It is hard to say how much of this is history and how much is an elaboration of the facts. In any case, according to Acts, it was on this journey that the entourage encountered the storm and endured a shipwreck. Paul was saved by the centurion from sure death when soldiers wanted to kill Paul so that he would not flee. He was imprisoned in Rome for two years (Acts 28:30) and continued to preach.

One tradition recounts that Paul actually got to Spain, although it is more likely that his imprisonment ended with his execution in Rome, probably in A.D. 62. (For a fuller account of Paul see "Paul" in *Harper's Bible Dictionary*.)

PAUL IN ROMANS	
Romans 12:14	Bless those who persecute you; bless and do not curse them.
Romans 12:16	Live in harmony with one another; do not be haughty, but associate with the lowly; do not claim to be wiser than you are.
Romans 12:17, 21	Do not repay anyone evil for evil, but take thought for what is noble in the sight of all. . . . Do not be overcome by evil, but overcome evil with good.
Romans 12:19b	. . . for it is written, "Vengeance is mine, I will repay, says the Lord."
Romans 12:20	No, "if your enemies are hungry, feed them; if they are thirsty, give them something to drink; for by doing this you will heap burning coals on their heads."
OLD TESTAMENT AND ORAL TRADITION	
Deuteronomy 32:35	Vengeance is mine, and recompense, for the time when their foot shall slip; because the day of their calamity is at hand, their doom comes swiftly.
Proverbs 3:7	Do not be wise in your own eyes; fear the Lord, and turn away from evil.
Proverbs 25:21-22	If your enemies are hungry, give them bread to eat; and if they are thirsty, give them water to drink; for you will heap coals of fire on their heads, and the Lord will reward you.
Matthew 5:39	But I say to you, Do not resist an evildoer. But if anyone strikes you on the right cheek, turn the other also; . . .
Matthew 5:44	But I say to you, Love your enemies and pray for those who persecute you . . .

5
1 Corinthians 1:18–2:5

Strange Wisdom

LEARNING MENU

Based on what you know about your class members, their needs and the ways in which they learn best, choose at least one learning activity from each of the three Dimensions.

Opening Prayer
O God,
whom we cannot love unless we love our neighbors,
remove hate and prejudice from us and from all people,
so that your children may be reconciled
with those we fear, resent, or threaten;
and live together in your peace;
through Jesus Christ our Lord. Amen.

(From *Book of Common Worship*, © 1993 Westminster/John Knox Press; page 100. Used by permission of Westminster/John Knox Press.)

Dimension 1: What Does the Bible Say?

(A) Answer Dimension 1 questions.

Consider the following as you answer the questions raised in Dimension 1, page 38 of the study book:

1. The Jews demanded signs and the Greeks desired wisdom (1 Corinthians 1:22).

2. Paul characterized Christ in these ways: (a) to the Jews a stumbling block, which literally means "a scandal" (23); (b) to the Gentiles, foolishness (23); (c) the power of God (24); (d) the wisdom of God (24, 30); (e) righteousness (30); (f) sanctification (30); (g) redemption (30); and (h) crucified! (1:23; 2:2).

3. Paul described himself as a preacher who did not use lofty words and flowery phrases, or emphasize the importance of wisdom. He reminded his readers that he only sought to demonstrate the Spirit and the power of God (1 Corinthians 2:1-5).

4. Paul's advice about boasting, expressed in the modern vernacular, might sound something like this: "Don't brag on yourself to God, but brag on God to everyone!" (1 Corinthians 1:29-31)

(B) Think about boasting.

Before the session:
- Provide several dictionaries. Include various editions.
- Provide at least one thesaurus.
- Provide Bibles in several versions.

When the activity begins:
- Write on chalkboard or a large piece of paper the following:
—Jeremiah 9:23-24
—"Boast" or "boasting"
—"Self-esteem"
—1 Corinthians 1:27-31
—1 Corinthians 15:31
- Boasting is usually seen as a negative action based on an inappropriate attitude! Is this always true? As students arrive invite them to locate and read the references above, as found in the Bible, the dictionaries, and/or the thesaurus.
- Lead a discussion about boasting, with the only ground rule being that what students say must be supported by at least one of the biblical references they have just read. Ask:
—What does it mean to boast? (Class members may have found varying definitions.)
—What does it mean to have self-esteem?
—What is the difference between boasting and expressing one's sense of self-esteem?
—What does Paul say about boasting?
—When is boasting wrong, according to Paul?
—Did Paul ever say that it is all right to boast? When?
—How can the class summarize what it has said about boasting?
—Would Paul agree?

Dimension 2:
What Does the Bible Mean?

(C) Write a sermon.

Before the session:
- Provide extra Bibles for those who may not have brought their own.
- Provide one piece of paper and a pencil for each of three groups. The study book suggests that in 1 Corinthians 1:18-25 Paul was setting forth three major points that he wanted his congregation to understand. This sounds like an outline for a sermon. In this activity the class will engage in writing a brief "three-point sermon," which Paul might have preached.

When the activity begins:
- Divide the class into three groups.
- Give each group one of the following references from 1 Corinthians: (1) 1:18 and 1:23; (2) 1:18 and 1:21; (3) 1:19, 22-25.
- The task for each group is twofold: (1) One person will read the passage aloud while the rest follow along; (2) the group will compose one paragraph that "preaches" what this Bible passage means. If the group has more than eight members, you may choose to divide into sub-groups of two or three persons for a few minutes to discuss the meaning of the assigned verses. For some help, refer the groups to the paragraph in the study book on page 39, which begins with "In 1 Corinthians 1:18-25. . ."
- When each group has completed its paragraph, the class will select one member to "preach" the agreed upon paragraph, and will reassemble for the "sermon."
- The selected members can find a place at the front, facing the class.
—Group 1 "preacher" will stand and begin by saying, "The first point of this sermon is this" and will follow by reading the group's paragraph.
—In similar fashion, groups 2 and 3 will "preach" their paragraphs.
- Initiate a discussion of the "sermon" by asking the class to give it a title.

(D) Sing 1 Corinthians 2:2.

Before the session begins:
- Provide enough hymnals so that the class can sing "Ask Ye What Great Thing I Know."
- Invite an accompanist to lead the singing.

When the activity begins:
- Share the following information: "The text of this hymn was written in 1741 by Johann C. Schwedler and is based on 1 Corinthians 2:2 and Galatians 6:14."

24

JOURNEY THROUGH THE BIBLE

- Read these two passages to the class.
- Ask students to scan the words and note the connection with the passages just read.
- Sing the entire hymn.
- Again sing the hymn, this time dividing the class into two groups. Group 1 should sing the questions. Group 2 should respond emphatically with "Jesus Christ, the crucified."
- Invite both groups to sing together the entire last stanza.
- The class may want to sing it again so that each group has sung both parts.

(E) Develop a "faith community."

TEACHING TIP

This activity poses the question: What is the difference, if any, between a faith community and other support groups or communities of which people may be a part? The activity begins with discussion, but its power lies with decisions the group may be led to make as a result of the discussion.

- Ask:
—Of what kinds of support groups are you aware? (These can be groups in which members are directly involved or ones of which they may simply know.)
- List support groups named on chalkboard or a piece of paper.
- Ask:
—What characteristics (that legitimately identify them as "support" groups) do these groups have in common?
- Again, list these on chalkboard or a piece of paper.
- Discuss:
—What are the characteristics of a "faith community"?
—In what ways are these similar to support groups?
—In what ways do they differ?
- Compare your ideas with those in the study book, Dimension 2, which refer to "faith community."
- Consider:
—How could this class help this faith community be more of what it could be? (Caution: If the class desires to act on these ideas, they should not do it "Lone Ranger" style, but initiate a discussion using decision-making structures already in place.)

(F) Examine the concept of "power."

- Share: The sidebar in the study book, "Wisdom in Corinth," (page 40) suggests that power is an end result. First comes a recognized skill; then status; followed by honor; "connections;" and finally power.
- Discuss:
—In the world today, what are the skills that seem to lead finally to power?
—Or, if skill is not now a starting point for power, what is?
—What did Paul say about human characteristics and "power" in 1 Corinthians 2:1-5?

(G) Be "agents" of God's love.

"Paul's gospel declares that life is a gift of God's love, and that it flourishes where God's people become agents of that love in and for the world" (page 41, study book). An agent may be defined as "one who is empowered to act for or represent another." There are several ways you may choose to lead the class in this activity.

Option One:
- Invite students to imagine that they are an employer who wants to hire "an agent for God's love." They will need to write a "Help Wanted" ad for the local newspaper. To do so, the following concerns should be considered:
—What personal characteristics will this agent need to possess?
—What previous experience?
—What job training is required?
—What are the benefits the employee may expect?
—What will be the agent's relationship to the CEO?
- After the class has suggested responses to these questions, divide the group into smaller units of two or three, asking each group to write a sample ad.
- Hear the ads that have been created. Let the class decide which is the most descriptive and which is the most creative. Have some fun with this!

Option Two:
- Instead of writing the ad, as described in Option One, plan a skit that will use the responses given by the class.

Before the session:
- Several days before the class session, invite a class member to be the job interviewer for those seeking the position of "agent of God's love."
- Provide for this person the list of questions in Option One so that they can be imagining the interview ahead of time. Do not provide any possible answers!
- Recruit two or three people who will agree to take part in a skit, but give them no more information. Just say, "Trust me!"
- If possible, arrange the classroom with a desk and two chairs as an interview area.

When the activity begins:
- Say to the class: "It just so happens that there actually is a job opening for an agent of God's love. Present with us today is (name, fictional or real), CEO of New Earth, Inc. who would like to interview applicants. [Interviewer takes a seat behind the desk.] If there is an applicant from this class, please step forward."
- Encourage others to apply and conduct interviews.

- After several applicant interviews, summarize the interviewing experience. Ask the interviewer:
—How did it feel to be interviewing for such an important position?
- Ask the interviewees:
—How did you feel before the interview?
—Why did you apply for this job?
—If you were to interview again, what would you do differently?
- Ask the class:
—What feelings or new learnings would you be willing to share?
—Is this a job for which you would like to apply? Why or why not?

Option Three:
- Begin this option with the discussion suggested at the beginning of Option One. Then divide the class into groups of four or five. Let each group choose an "interviewer."
- Have copies of the interview questions prepared ahead of time, one for each interviewer.
- Let each group proceed as an interview session, with members of the group serving as job applicants, one at a time.
- Reassemble the class, and continue with a summarizing discussion as suggested at the close of Option Two.

Dimension 3: What Does the Bible Mean to Us?

(H) Compare hymns about the cross.

Before the session:
- Provide hymnals that contain "The Old Rugged Cross" (No. 504, *The United Methodist Hymnal*) and "In the Cross of Christ I Glory" (No. 295).
- Invite an accompanist to lead your hymns.

When the activity begins:
- Begin a discussion of the cross by asking the group to sing "The Old Rugged Cross." After singing ask these questions:
—What memories does this hymn recall for you?
—What does it say to you about the meaning of the cross?
—What is the feeling with which you are left after singing this hymn?
- Continue the discussion by leading the class in singing "In the Cross of Christ I Glory."
- Repeat the three questions above.
—How would you describe the difference between these two hymns?
—In the focus Scripture passage for this session, what did Paul say that this passage did not say about the cross and Christ's death?
—What did Paul say?
—Which of these hymns do you think Paul might have chosen as his "favorite"?

(I) Describe two meanings of *success*.

—How does the world define *success*?
—What did Paul say about "success"?
- Divide the class into two groups.
- Ask group 1 to describe success.
- Ask Group 2 to define success. Suggest that in preparation for the discussion the group read 1 Corinthians 1:26–2:5.
- Reassemble, hear the reports, and discuss.
- Summarize by asking someone to read aloud the Scripture reference above. Follow this with reading aloud the last two paragraphs of the study book, Dimension 3, page 44, beginning with "This, of course, is the apostle's point."

(J) Face a tough question.

According to the study book, page 44, success means "embracing the status that is already ours by reason of God's gift of life." The suggestion is that we not try to "get ahead" of others, but those who are "ahead" should be affirmed by us.
- To stimulate thinking about some difficult issues, try asking the following questions:
—What is the message of the cross for the oppressed?
—the homeless?
—the victims of poverty?
—the victims of physical or emotional abuse?
—How do these people affirm others "in love"?
—Is there a message of the cross for those who are the privileged of our society?

(K) Write it down.

- Try to capture in your notebook the feelings you have had during this session. Write a statement that summarizes for you the meaning of the title given for this session, "Strange Wisdom."

Additional Bible Helps

The City of Corinth
The city of Corinth was founded in the tenth century B.C. at the southwest end of a narrow isthmus that connected mainland Greece with the Peloponnesus. So strategic was the location that it became an important route for both military and commercial travel. By 400 B.C. the population

may have numbered over 100,000. In 146 B.C. it was destroyed by Roman armies, people were killed or taken into slavery, and the city was burned. Only a remnant poor lived at the site for the next one hundred years.

A City Repopulated With Slaves
In 44 B.C. Julius Caesar refounded the city, populating it with many poor and former slaves. In less than twenty years it was named the capital of Achaia and continued as an important commercial settlement through the Middle Ages.

The city that Paul knew had once again gained prominence and population, becoming an important urban center. The population may have been 130,000, exceeding the number of residents at the time of its destruction in 146 B.C. While most people spoke Greek, names in the New Testament associated with Corinth are about one-half Greek and one-half Latin. As an official Roman colony, Latin was its official language.

House Churches
Excavations at ancient sites indicate that people lived in small villas, which would have limited the number of people who could worship in the house churches. Factions among the Christians at Corinth may have been increased, in part, by this separation of the church into these smaller units. Rows of small shops, probably like the one that Paul shared with tentmaker Aquila, have also been excavated.

Many deities and cults were part of the religious life of Corinth at the time of Paul. Prominent among the deities was the god, Apollo and the goddess, Athena. Also important was Tyche, the goddess of good fortune, and Aphrodite, the goddess of love, fertility, and beauty.

Even in ancient times Corinth had the reputation of being a city of sexual orgies and excesses. However, recent scholarship suggests that Corinth of Paul's day was probably no more or no less "immoral" than any of the other port cities of the Mediterranean world.

Leaders in the Church at Corinth
In Paul's ministry with the church at Corinth, he was assisted, from time to time, by Silvanus and Timothy. Other leaders within the church mentioned by Paul included Prisca (Priscilla) and Aquila, Achaicus, Fortunatus, Stephanas, Crispus and Gaius, Phoebe, and Erastus.

The members of the church were primarily Gentile, although some had a Jewish background, with a special interest in religious knowledge.

Apollos
From the Book of Acts we learn about Apollos, the man (Acts 18:24–19:1); from Paul's letter to the church at Corinth we learn how Paul perceived Apollos' ministry in relation to his own (1 Corinthians 3:5-9).

Apollos was a Jew, a native of Alexandria. He was well-versed in the Scriptures, had been instructed in the "Way of the Lord," and had received the "baptism of John." In his preaching he refuted the Jews, and showed through his interpretation of Scripture that Jesus was the long-awaited Messiah. He preached in the synagogue at Ephesus, eloquently and enthusiastically. With the encouragement of the Christians in Ephesus, he went on to Corinth to continue his preaching.

A Baptism of Repentance
With Paul's first arrival in Ephesus, he discovered that Apollos had been there before him, baptizing in the name of John. Paul explained that this baptism was a call to repentance, in preparation for the One who was to come after John, namely Jesus. When Paul baptized them again, this time in the name of Jesus, the writer of Acts reported that "the Holy Spirit came upon them and they spoke in tongues and prophesied" (Acts 19:6).

A Message to a Divided Church
Paul's message to a divided church in Corinth is recorded in 1 Corinthians. Although Paul was the founder of the church, a new preacher had come among them, one with eloquence as an orator and enthusiasm for his message. It would have been human nature for Paul to jealously strike out at Apollos as a rival and competitor. Instead, he spoke of Apollos in collegial terms, and turned his displeasure toward the people in Corinth for having chosen up sides— some for Paul and some for Apollos.

Paul insisted that both he and Apollos were simply servants of God. He reminded them that they had come to faith through the preaching of Apollos as well as his own. He had introduced them to Christ, and the preaching of Apollos had helped the church grow. He cautioned them not to forget, however, that while he "planted" and Apollos "watered," it was God who had given the growth (1 Corinthians 3:6)!

(For further insights read *Harper's Bible Dictionary*, "Corinth," "Apollos"; *The Anchor Bible*, "II Corinthians," (pages 4-22).

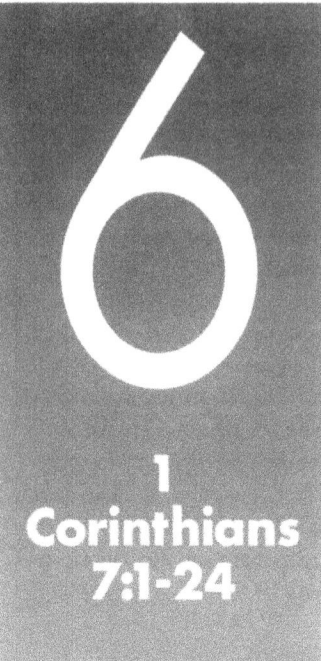

6 Particular Gifts

1 Corinthians 7:1-24

LEARNING MENU

Based on what you know about your class members, their needs, and the ways in which they learn best, choose at least one learning activity from each of the three Dimensions.

Opening Prayer
Gracious God,
you have called us to be the church of Jesus Christ.
Keep us one in faith and service,
breaking bread together,
and proclaiming the good news to the world,
that all may believe you are love,
turn to your ways,
and live in the light of your truth;
through Jesus Christ our Lord. Amen.

(From *Book of Common Worship*, © 1993 Westminster/John Knox Press; page 100. Used by permission of Westminster/John Knox Press.)

TEACHING TIPS

Looking Ahead
While preparing this session, look ahead at the activities for session 7. If you plan to use activity (H) next week, you will need to make a request of your class members. Ask them to bring to the next session of the class a picture of someone who was for them an example of how to live.

Suggestions for Leading the Session
As the leader for this session you will want to be sensitive to the feelings of the group members. Some of your class members may give the impression of being nonchalant about discussions of sex-related issues, all the while living with deep hurts and anxieties. Most will have experienced divorce, either their own or that of some member of their family. Some, even at this moment, may be experiencing difficulties in their marriage, which they have shared with no one.

The intention of this session is to highlight sexual attitudes and admonitions in the New Testament and to ask what this means for people in today's world. It is not the intention that this session become uncomfortable for anyone, or that it give the appearance of therapy. Remember:

- You can be relaxed in talking about sexual issues without being flippant. (This is not a time for jokes.)
- You can accept feelings without labeling them as "good" or "bad." ("Thank you for sharing" is all you may need to say.)
- You can suggest or encourage the expression of another point of view without labeling the one just shared as "right" or "wrong." (You can ask, "Does anyone have a similar idea or a different idea about this?")

- You can accept and appreciate personal experiences that are offered without asking for or insisting on more specific information. (If class members press for details, you can intervene with, "Let's let her comment stand now, just as it is. Perhaps at a later time she will want to say more.")
- You can respect a silent member's silence without insisting on verbal participation.
- You can suggest your willingness to talk further with a concerned person at a later time without implying that what has already been said was inappropriate. ("We need to move on now, Seth, but I'll be glad to talk with you further after class.")

Dimension 1: What Does the Bible Say?

(A) Answer Dimension 1 questions.

1. The conditions under which Christian spouses may abstain from sexual relations include these: (1) decision to do so by mutual agreement; (2) the decision to do so for a temporary period of time; and (3) the time thus set aside would be used for prayer.

2. In 1 Corinthians 7:10 Paul attributed to the Lord this admonition: A wife should not separate from her husband, but if she does, she should remain unmarried or be reconciled to her husband. On the other hand, the only admonition in this passage for the husband is that he should not divorce his wife.

3. Paul believed that a marriage can work even though only one spouse is a Christian. The non-Christian spouse in such a marriage is made holy, or sanctified, not by the marriage but by the action of God. (1 Corinthians 7:12-14)

4. Whether one is a Jewish Christian or a Gentile Christian, circumcised or uncircumcised, is nothing. Obeying the commandments of God is everything.

(B) Compare Bible passages about divorce.

Before the session:
- Write these references on chalkboard or a large sheet of paper: (1) Matthew 5:32; 19:9; (2) Mark 10:6-12; (3) Luke 16:18; (4) Deuteronomy 24:1-4; (5) 1 Corinthians 7:10-11. (Circle the Corinthians reference.)
The sidebar titled, "Jesus and Divorce," found in the study book, places these references in their chronological context. This activity compares Paul's statement on divorce with those found in Deuteronomy and the Gospels.

When the activity begins:
- Divide the class into four groups, or if the class is large, into groups that are multiples of four.
- Assign to each group either the Deuteronomy passage or one of the Gospel passages.
- Assign the Corinthians passage to each group.
- Each group should read the assigned passages, compare the Old Testament or Gospel reference with 1 Corinthians, and prepare to report their findings.
- Hear the reports; discuss the differences found in the references read; summarize by reviewing the study book comments on "Jesus and Divorce."

Dimension 2: What Does the Bible Mean?

(C) Continue with activity (B).

- If activity (B) above was chosen, you may want to continue with this question:
—Taken all together, does the Bible say anything with certainty about the subject of divorce?

(D) Decide how to decide.

In the matter of sexual ethics, how does one decide? One way is to adopt a set of rules, and follow them absolutely, regardless of the situation. Another way is to adopt a principle which can be applied afresh to each situation. In 1966, Joseph Fletcher (see sidebar "Six Ethical Propositions") created a stir when he wrote that one should enter into every decision-making situation "fully armed with the ethical maxims of [his] community and its heritage, and... treat them with respect as illuminators of [his] problems... prepared in any situation to compromise them or set them aside *in the situation* if love seems better served by doing so" (page 26). The author of the study book writes that Paul "recognized that individual situations vary, and that what is appropriate in one instance may not be in another."

- Write the preceding quotations side by side on a large sheet of paper.
- Ask the following questions:
—What are the ethical maxims of our Judeo-Christian heritage as we find them in the Bible? (See activities (B) and (C).)
—What are the ethical maxims of this faith community?
—Should we live by specific rules, or by principles which are applied anew to each situation?
—What principle(s) would be appropriate?
—What are the dangers of each approach?

> **Six Ethical Propositions**
>
> 1. Only one "thing" is intrinsically good, namely, love (page 57).
> 2. The ruling norm of Christian decisions is love (page 69).
> 3. Love and justice are the same, for justice is love distributed (page 87).
> 4. Love wills the neighbor's good whether we like [him] or not (page 103).
> 5. Only the end justifies the means; nothing else (page 120).
> 6. Love's decisions are made situationally, not pre-scriptively (page 134).
>
> (*Situation Ethics*, by Joseph Fletcher; Westminster Press, 1966)

(E) Compare "then" and "now."

> **TEACHING TIP**
>
> **Looking Ahead**
> The meaning of the Bible for our time is complicated by the cultural distance between "then" and "now." This activity is in two parts. The first will help class members personally feel the differences made by the passing of time. The second may help shed new light on the difficulty of discerning biblical meanings.

Step One:
- On chalkboard or a large sheet of paper provide three columns; label them, "THEN," "THEN," and "NOW."
- Ask:
—In two or three words, what was the world like in our grandparents' time? (Enter replies in the second "THEN" column.)
- Ask:
—What is our world like today? (Enter these replies under "NOW.")
- Discuss:
—How is it different today when making decisions than it must have been in our grandparents' time?

Step Two:
- Follow the procedure in Step One.
- Ask:
—In a few words, what was the world like in Paul's time and place? (Enter these replies in the first "THEN" column.)
- Look again at the "NOW" entries. Ask if there is anything that needs to be added in that column.
- Discuss:
—How is it different today when making decisions than it must have been in Paul's day?

—How is it the same today?
—How do these similarities and differences affect how we go about making ethical decisions today?

Dimension 3: What Does the Bible Mean to Us?

(F) Find truth in the comics.

- The comic pages of the newspaper reveal a lot about our values, as well as our sense of humor! How many different assumptions about family and sexual values can be found in the "funnies"? Have some fun with this! Reading some of the comics to the class might be a lighthearted way to begin the serious discussions in Dimension 3.

(G) Continue with activities (B) and (C).

- If activities (B) and (C) above were chosen, you may want to continue with this question:
—What do these statements from the Bible about divorce mean for us today?

(H) List sexual dilemmas of the twentieth and twenty-first centuries.

- Share:
  In the focus Scripture passage for this session, Paul was responding to specific questions that had apparently been addressed to him in a letter that has not been preserved.
- List on a large sheet of paper or chalkboard questions that might be in a letter addressed to Paul, if written today. Consider two options for this method:
—(1) Simply leave questions in view of the class during the remainder of the session. Members may refer back to them in subsequent discussions. If not, don't insist.
—(2) Provide opportunity for discussion if class members seem anxious to talk about these questions.

(I) Live as in the presence of God.

- Consider this statement from the study book, page 45: "What really matters [according to Paul] . . . is whether, whatever the particular situation, one lives as in the presence of God." (This activity will help class members discover for themselves the meaning of living "as in the presence of God.")
- Without using the above paragraph as introduction, divide the class into two or more groups.
- Assign each group the task of describing briefly a present-day ethical dilemma, written in narrative form. Appropriate to this session would be an ethical dilemma related to sexual behavior, although this is not necessary.

- Ask groups to exchange dilemmas. Explain that each group is to suggest actions or attitudes that would be appropriate for the "characters" in the dilemma they have been given. Their only guideline is that the characters should make their choices as if "in the presence of God."
- Reassemble the class.
- First, ask how groups interpreted the meaning of "as in the presence of God." Help members resist the temptation to speak specifically about the assigned dilemma.
- Next, ask each group to read its assigned dilemma, and the agreed upon resolution.
- Finally, help the group summarize this activity by identifying any decision-making principles that have emerged through this process.

(J) Ponder a question about love.

- Consider the following concern:
— If "love" is agreed upon as a basic principle to be followed when making decisions related to sex, who determines which behaviors are then appropriate and acceptable?

(K) Compare cultural values by watching television.

Before the session:
- Videotape a recently produced TV family situation comedy.
- Also, videotape a similar program produced twenty or thirty years ago. (Reruns are abundant!) You may choose to stop the taping during the commercials.
- Arrange to have video playback equipment in your classroom.

When the activity begins:
- View first the currently produced program.
- Questions for discussion might include the following:
—In what kind of world is today's TV family living?
—What are the problems they face?
—What seem to be the guidelines for sexual behavior?
—What constitutes a "family"?
- Next, view the "yesterday" video.
- Questions for discussion might include the following:
—In what kind of world was "yesterday's" TV family living?
—How were their problems different from today's TV family?
—How was "family" described then?

TEACHING TIP

Many people feel that we unthinkingly accept as normal the family values depicted in television. This activity can help your class members compare the family life depicted today with that of one or two generations ago.

(L) Compare sexual values by listening to recordings.

Before the session:
- Secure a recording of the Top Ten popular songs of thirty years ago. Look in your own collection, a friend's collection, the local library, or a record shop.
- Find copies of the current top vocal recordings.
- Arrange to have playback equipment in the classroom.

When the activity begins:
Although we may sing to express who we are, it is also possible that we may become what we sing!
- Play one or two of the songs recorded thirty years ago.
- Ask:
—What are the accepted sexual values imbedded in these songs?
- Play one or two of the songs currently at the top of the charts.
- Ask:
—What are the sexual values in these songs?
—How generally do you think these values are accepted today?
- Compare with songs from an earlier day.
- Discuss the experience of listening.
—If Paul were asked to comment on today's values, how might he respond?

(M) Read "advice columns" from Paul's point of view.

- Before the session find letters in the "advice" column of your local paper that deal with issues of marriage and divorce.
- Create an informal dramatization. Let someone play the part of Paul, the "advice columnist," who is just opening his mail. He reads aloud a "letter" just received, and asks the class for help in answering it.
- Refer the class to the section in the study book, "Jesus and Divorce," page 49.
- After the class has "helped Paul" with its understanding of Jesus' point of view, let "Paul" think aloud about his own point of view, answering the letter by putting into his own words the final paragraph of Dimension 2 in the study book, page 50.

(N) Sing a prayer for acceptance.

- Consider closing this session with the hymn, "Help Us Accept Each Other" (*The United Methodist Hymnal*, No. 560).
- Ask:
—What does it mean to accept each other?
- Invite class members to respond with one- or two-word answers.
—What does it mean when we say Christ has accepted us?

(Again, encourage brief answers.)
— Who are some of the people in our world whom we find difficult to accept?
• Sing all verses of the hymn.

> **Optional Method**
> Instead of group singing, ask someone to sing the hymn as a solo. This will make it possible to form a circle, holding hands, while listening to the words and music of the hymn.

(O) Write it down.

• You may want to give the class time to write in their notebooks before they leave class. If not, encourage them to do so at their earliest convenience. Once again, assure members that these comments are for their own use. They will at no time be asked to share them, although they are free to volunteer insights they have gained through this activity.

Additional Bible Helps

The Holy Kiss
References to "the holy kiss" are found in four of Paul's letters: Romans 16:16; 1 Corinthians 16:20; 2 Corinthians 13:12; and 1 Thessalonians 5:26. The "holy kiss" was a greeting exchanged between Christians, and may have been a liturgical element of early Christian worship. Its use was perhaps an intentional attempt to begin to create symbols and rituals that would in turn build up a sense of community among the early Christians. It also served as a public statement that the Christians were no longer divided by gender or condition of servitude, but were united in Christ. (See Galatians 3:28.) The several references to the "holy kiss" by Paul would seem to make it clear that this was a practice he both supported and encouraged.

It should be noted that the "holy kiss" is to be contrasted with several other kinds of kisses referred to in the Bible. For example, there is the kiss upon leaving a friend (1 Samuel 20:41 and 2 Samuel 19:39). Or, there is the kiss upon greeting or taking leave of close relatives (Genesis 29:11; 31:28; or Exodus 4:27). There is the purely erotic kiss of Proverbs 7:13 and Song of Solomon 1:2; 8:1. Finally, there is the kiss of betrayal (2 Samuel 20:9; Matthew 26:49; Mark 14:45; and Luke 22:47). In some religious communities the "holy kiss" continues as a sign of Christian love and unity.

Paul and the Teachings of Jesus
A discussion of Paul's use of Jesus' teachings must necessarily be prefaced by a reminder that in all probability, all of Paul's letters preserved in our New Testament were written prior to the writing of the Gospel of Mark. Since Mark is generally accepted as the earliest of the Gospels, this raises the question of how Paul may have received any of Jesus' sayings. There are two possibilities.

One way that Paul might have received some of the sayings of Jesus would have been through a written collection of those sayings, circulated in the first century, but no longer in existence.

Second, and most plausible, is that Paul, in all likelihood, was well aware of a rich, oral tradition that existed within the Christian community. There were no computer networks or databases in the first century! There was, however, a culture adept at remembering important events and sayings, and a network of relationships through which these events and sayings were passed on by word of mouth from village to village and from generation to generation.

Twice in Paul's letters it seems clear that he referred to specific, known sayings of Jesus. First, there is the discussion of divorce in 1 Corinthians 7:10-11. Paul wrote, "not I, but the Lord," indicating that the instruction was from Jesus.

Second, in 1 Corinthians 9 Paul discussed his right, as well as his refusal, to accept living expenses from the Corinthians. His appeal to validate this principle was to Jesus when he wrote, "In the same way, the Lord commanded that those who proclaim the gospel should get their living by the gospel." (See 1 Corinthians 9:14 as well as Matthew 10:10 and Luke 10:7.) However, Paul also noted that this is a "right," not a demand, and that one is free to give up a "right."

More difficult to document is the possibility that Paul was knowingly using sayings of Jesus without reference to "the Lord" as their source. Part of this difficulty stems from the fact that some of the Jesus tradition is similar to other first century teachings. It is also conceivable that Paul knew some of the sayings as teachings of the early church, but did not know them as coming specifically from Jesus.

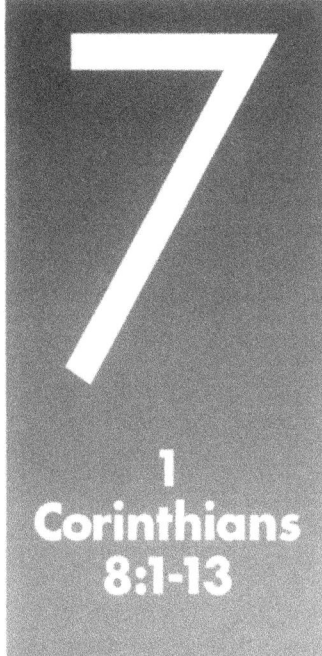

NECESSARY KNOWLEDGE

1 Corinthians 8:1-13

LEARNING MENU

Based on what you know about your class members, their needs and the ways in which they learn best, choose at least one learning activity from each of the three Dimensions.

Opening Prayer
Eternal God,
our beginning and our end,
be our starting point and our haven,
and accompany us in this day's journey.
Use our hands to do the work of your creation,
and use our lives to bring others the new life you give
this world in Jesus Christ, Redeemer of all. Amen.

(From *Book of Common Worship*, © 1993 Westminster/John Knox Press; page 500. Used by permission of Westminster/John Knox Press.)

Dimension 1: What Does the Bible Say?

(A) Answer Dimension 1 questions.

Answers to questions from the study book include the following:

1. 1 Corinthians 8:6 is a two-part affirmation because the truth it expresses is two-fold. For others there may be many gods, but for Christians there is "one God, the Father," and "one Lord, Jesus Christ."

2. Not everyone understands that, in spite of the many gods worshiped by people, there is only one God (1 Corinthians 8:4-7).

3. For Paul, eating meat offered to idols did not defile the Christian as long as it was understood that these pagan sacrifices had no power. So, whether one ate such meat or not was of no consequence. However, the "weak" were those who were ill-informed about the faith and inexperienced in the Christian life. They still believed that there was power in these pagan sacrifices (1 Corinthians 8:7).

4. If those who understood that the idols had no power were seen eating in a pagan temple, it might suggest to some other Christian with less understanding that Christians believe in the power of idols.

(B) Prepare for a church dinner.

Food is a basic need of both animals and humans. Eating at a place of worship is a religious tradition of long-standing. Whether they are called "covered dish," "take in," "carry in," or "potluck," most of us have had to decide what food to take to church, and how to prepare it.

- Ask class members to recall a church supper for which they prepared a "dish to pass."

—What were all of the questions they had to answer before they could decide what to take? (They may suggest some of these: How many dishes will I take? What will it be? How much money should I spend? What will people eat? For health reasons should I avoid cholesterol, fat, sugar, or salt? What about people's allergies? Few Protestant Christians will cite biblical or denominational dietary rules. (See the sidebar, "Religious Dietary Restrictions.")
- In Paul's time there were also questions about what foods were acceptable to eat and questions about eating in places of worship. Ask the class to find these questions in 1 Corinthians 8:1-13 and 10:23-30.
—How did Paul solve these questions for himself?
—Was this a good solution?

Religious Dietary Restrictions

Two Christian groups with dietary restrictions are the Roman Catholic Church and the Seventh Day Adventist Church, but each has a different focus.

Roman Catholic Church

In the Roman Catholic Church of the United States, there are two types of dietary regulations: abstinence and fasting. These dietary restrictions are limited to the days of Lent, and complying with these is one of the spiritual disciplines of the season. Ash Wednesday and all of the Fridays of Lent are designated as days of abstinence: no meat will be eaten. Ash Wednesday and Good Friday, in addition to being days of abstinence, are also days of fasting: only one, regular meal will be eaten.

Seventh Day Adventist Church

For Seventh Day Adventists dietary restrictions are not limited to one season of the Christian year. Nor are they only a spiritual discipline. The regulations about food are for every day, and a primary concern is one of health. They cite the biblical record that God's original diet for humans was seed-bearing plants and fruits (Genesis 1:29). After the Fall, plants of the field were added (Genesis 3:18). This vegetarian diet is considered as the ideal. Pork and shellfish are seen as "unclean," because they contain toxins and contaminants sometimes poisonous to human beings. These "unclean" meats are forbidden. While "clean" meats are not forbidden, a strict vegetarian diet is still seen as the healthy ideal. (*Seventh Day Adventists Believe...*, Ministerial Association, General Conference of Seventh Day Adventists, Washington, D.C., 1988; pages 284-86.)

Dimension 2: What Does the Bible Mean?

(C) Know God in two ways.

The study book makes a distinction between *knowledge about God*, and *knowledge of God*. This activity, in two steps, will help students understand the difference between these two terms.

Step One:
- On chalkboard or large sheets of paper (you may need three pieces, side by side) create three columns. Name the center column "God is..."; for the moment, do not name the other two columns.
- Ask class members to suggest two or three word phrases that describe what God is like. Record responses in the center column.

Step Two:
- At this point, label column one, "Knowledge about" and column three, "Knowledge of."
- Read aloud, or refer to the study book paragraph that begins, "In verses 1b-3. . . ." (page 56)
- Return to the first item mentioned and ask, "How do we know this about God?" Record the answer reported in the appropriate column. There is no right answer here. The examples below illustrate that persons may come to their understanding of God in different ways.

Knowledge about...	God is...	Knowledge of...
Reading the Bible	Creator	Felt God's presence on a wilderness trip.
Sunday school book	Forgiveness	I just knew I had been forgiven.

(D) Know God through experiencing God's love.

- Share the statement, "We know of God through the experience of God's love."
- Divide the class into pairs.
- Ask each, in turn, to share how they have experienced God's love, or how someone they know has experienced God's love.
- Call the group back together and acknowledge that for some this may be the first time they have talked with another person about their own experience of God.
- Encourage them to share how they felt about this process.

(E) Identify your "rights."

Paul asserted that Christians have a right to eat meat from pagan sacrifices, since they know that the pagan idols have

no power in their lives. But he also suggested that sometimes "rights" should be given up, for the sake of other people. Help the class identify "rights" contemporary people have today that they might choose not to exercise.
• Share this discussion starter:

> On your way to work the car you are driving is sideswiped by another car. Fortunately, you are not hurt. You get the license number, and as you watch, the car careens down the street, narrowly missing another car and running the traffic light at the next corner. You are shocked, angry, and concerned about the safety of others.
>
> On investigation you discover that the driver's insurance policy has lapsed. You think, "I'm going to sue! I have a right to sue!" However, you further discover that the driver was a frantic mother, whose one-year-old baby was choking on a small toy he had swallowed. She was trying to get him to a nearby hospital emergency room. What should you do? You have a right to sue for damages. But Paul would say that you are not required to insist upon that right.

• Ask:
—What other "rights" do you have and under what circumstances might we not insist upon those rights?

(F) Find out how Paul felt about eating meat.

• Before the session, recruit four people to read the script "Paul Talks About Meat."(See the dialogue box, pages 35-36.) Paul did not have a set of rules that he applied to every situation, regardless of the circumstances. He listened to the questions he was asked and often responded in the light of individual circumstances. Such was the case when asked about eating meat that had been offered as a sacrifice to pagan idols.
• Set up an office for "Paul." His office sign might read, "Paul, Meat Consultant." The scene begins with Paul sitting at his desk.
• THE SHOPPER enters as the dialogue begins.
• When the dialogue concludes, ask class members to summarize what Paul said about eating meat that had been sacrificed to idols.
—How many modern issues can the class identify for which solutions must take into account specific existing circumstances?

Paul Talks About Meat

Characters:
PAUL, THE SHOPPER, THE DINNER GUEST, THE TEMPLE DINER

Setting:
PAUL'S OFFICE

(The Shopper knocks)
PAUL: Come on in! I'm just finishing up some correspondence to the Philippians. Here, sit down. You look like you've been on the road for quite a while.
SHOPPER: I'm The Shopper. I've just come from Corinth with a question for you about eating meat. I'm a Christian, you know.
PAUL: Good, good . . . .
SHOPPER: Well, my wife keeps sending me to the market to buy meat, and I don't know. You look at the meat, but you can't tell where it's come from, or for that matter, what god it has been sacrificed to! I think we ought to find these things out, but my wife keeps saying: "Just buy the meat! Don't ask questions!" I keep making a fuss about it, until, well. . .to tell you the truth, she just kicked me out of the house. She said, "Go find Paul, and don't come back until you get a straight answer!" So, after many days walking those dusty roads, here I am!
PAUL: Look, Shopper, you and I. . . we know those pagan gods don't really exist, and if they did, they would have no power over us. Sorry you had such a long trip, but your wife is right. Just go to the market, buy the best looking meat you can find there and at the best price, and don't ask questions!
SHOPPER: Thanks. Sorry to have troubled you. (As he leaves he mutters, "Sure hate to have to tell her she was right . . . well, I'll think of something.)"
(The Dinner Guest knocks.)
PAUL: Come on in.
DINNER GUEST: I'm The Dinner Guest. Sorry to trouble you, sir, but I've come a long way. . . from Corinth, as you may have guessed. . . with a very troublesome query. I'm a Christian, you know.
PAUL: Good, good. . .
DINNER GUEST: I was invited to a grand dinner at the home of a friend, a pagan, I fear. I was quite worried about eating meat in his home, not knowing whether it had been sacrificed to a pagan idol.
PAUL: You didn't ask him, did you?
DINNER GUEST *(hesitantly)*: Well, no. . .
PAUL: Good, good! The last person here was asking about meat, and I told him the same thing I'm going to tell you: Just don't ask! Don't worry about it. Just eat and enjoy!
DINNER GUEST: Well, all right, I didn't ask. But before I knew it, he volunteered that it had come from a pagan temple!
PAUL: Uh oh! So what did you do? (I'm afraid to ask!)
DINNER GUEST: Well, I ate it anyway, since I don't believe in those idols.
PAUL: Now, there is where you made your mistake. Once you knew where it came from, you should have said, "Thanks, but no thanks."

DINNER GUEST: Really? Well, thanks, Paul. *(leaves muttering)* But no thanks!
(The Temple Diner knocks.)
PAUL: Come on in. It isn't about eating meat, is it?
TEMPLE DINER: As a matter of fact. . .
PAUL: All right, what's the question?
TEMPLE DINER: My name is The Temple Diner, and, I'm a Christian, you know.
PAUL: Good, good.
TEMPLE DINER: But I have a lot of pagan friends and relatives, and there's this big wedding in a couple of months at the pagan temple. Of course, after the wedding there'll be a wonderful banquet in the temple dining room. They need to know how many will be there for the banquet, so I have to reply soon. But I didn't want to do something wrong. I thought I should ask you. Will it be all right for me to eat in the temple dining room?
PAUL: You're from Corinth, aren't you? This has all the earmarks of a Corinthian question! Look, Diner, eating in that pagan temple won't hurt you. You know that, and I know that. But, how about some of the other guests? Maybe there will be recent converts to Christianity at that banquet. If they see you, a devout Christian, eating in the temple dining room, they may think that you find some religious significance in eating the temple meat. Then they'll eat it, and fall back into pagan ways. Of course, you have a right to eat it, but for the sake of others who may misunderstand, you should just go to the wedding, but decline the banquet invitation.
TEMPLE DINER: Well, if you say so, but they have such good meat at those temple banquets. . . .

Dimension 3: What Does the Bible Mean to Us?

Looking Ahead
Before this class session, look ahead to session 8. Scan the suggested activities. If you plan to use activity (K) you will need to prepare your class during this session.
• Encourage students to talk with at least one person before the next session, preferably not from this church, asking this question:
—How would you complete the sentence, *The church for me is. . . .*?
• Ask students to come to class next week a few minutes early. They should stop someone on their way into the building, preferably not someone from this class, and ask them the same question. They will be asked to share their findings during session 8.

(G) Practice making moral judgments.

"Moral judgments must be based on an assessment of motives, intentions, and consequences . . ." (study book, page 59). What does this formula look like if applied to some hotly debated moral discussions of our time, all of them a matter of life or death?
• Choose one topic to be discussed with the entire class. Or divide the class, giving a different topic to each smaller group. Or discuss more than one issue as an entire class, as the time permits.
Possible topics:
—Abortion. Pro-choice versus Anti-abortion;
—Participation in the military. Pro-military versus Conscientious objection;
—Capital punishment. Those for versus Those against;
—Terminal illness. Right to die versus Right to life;
• It is unlikely that the class will arrive at a unanimous opinion on any of these issues! Even so, consider these questions:
—Did the "motives-intentions-consequences" provide a helpful framework for the discussion?
—While acknowledging that we have much more information about all of these issues than was available to Paul, do you have any idea how Paul might have decided?

(H) Share stories of influential people.

Before the session:
• Class members have been asked to bring a picture of someone who has been for them an example of how to live.
• Provide hymnals and an instrumentalist.

When the activity begins:
• Divide the class into groups of no more than ten persons.
• Give each person three minutes to show the picture they brought and to describe how, through example, this person has been a life influence.
• Consider:
—How important is "example"? Paul thought it was so important that he would not eat meat lest a new convert follow his example and fall back into pagan ways. Is "example" still an important influence?
• Summarize the discussion by listing the values or qualities of life now claimed by class members, that have been encouraged and reinforced by others.
• Sing together the hymn, "I Sing a Song of the Saints of God" (*The United Methodist Hymnal*, No. 712).

(I) Help people grow in faith.

The purpose of this activity is to develop a set of guidelines for helping modern persons grow in the Christian faith. The guidelines will not come from faith development theorists, but from the life experiences of members of the class.

Before the activity:
Distribute a single piece of typing paper (8 1/2 by 11) to each student.

During the session:
- Direct students to hold the paper horizontally; then ask them to draw a line horizontally from one side of the page to the other across the top, labeling the left end of the line "Birth" and the right end of the line "Now."
- Ask students to think about their life, from birth to this present moment. How many major life stages can they identify? Mark off these stages on the lifeline and label them. There is no "right" way to do this. Each person's life is his or her own. Tell students that they will not be asked to share these worksheets.
- Now ask students to think about each stage.
—What were the life experiences during each period that helped them grow in their Christian faith? Students should enter these in the appropriate column of the worksheet.
- Write on chalkboard or paper: "HOW TO HELP PEOPLE GROW IN THE CHRISTIAN FAITH".
- Growing out of the worksheets just completed, lead the class in developing a set of guidelines for helping people grow in their faith.

(J) Write it down.

- Remind members to write in their notebooks while the session events are still fresh. What important new ideas or feelings have resulted from this session? Since this is about midway in this unit of study, suggest that they reread the notebook for any new insights it might offer.

Additional Bible Helps

Knowledge and Love
In 1 Corinthians 8:1 Paul contrasted knowledge and love. He seemed to play one against the other when he said "knowledge puffs up" but "love builds up." This apparent minimizing of the importance of knowledge has been used sometimes by those who want to downplay the importance of education; all that one needs is faith in Jesus Christ. Paul was not opposed to knowledge in general, but was distressed by the arrogant way in which some in Corinth seemed to be flaunting their religious knowledge.

Problems in the Corinthian Church
Any temptation to idealize the early Christian church vanishes when the church at Corinth is examined. Major problems and differences of opinion among the Corinthian Christians centered around the issues of sexual behavior, eating meat sacrificed to idols, and spiritual gifts, including prophecy and the speaking in tongues. These are the central topics of sessions 6, 7, and 8. There were other problems, perhaps less significant, to which Paul also felt a need to direct his attention.

"The Incestuous Man"
First Corinthians 5:1-5 describes a scenario in which a man was living with his stepmother. Since such a marriage was forbidden by both Roman and Jewish law, it is probable that they were not married, but simply cohabiting. However, Paul considered this to be a case of gross immorality, and he could not understand why the church had not long ago expelled this man from the church community. Verse 5 is troubling, as it seems to leave this man to suffer and to die without any support from the faith community. It has been noted that Paul's concern would appear to be more for the purity of the church than for the well-being of the offender.

The Use of Pagan Courts
Verses 1-8 describe another situation in which Paul called upon the church to act. Members had taken their grievances against each other to pagan courts, but Paul insisted that legal problems within the Christian community should have been solved by the assembled community itself. Better yet, such problems could have been avoided, had no wrongs been done. Problematic, here, is the issue of jurisdiction. What "wrongs" did the religious community have a right and obligation to solve, and which were a matter of secular law, outside the jurisdiction of the church?

Disorders
Once again the Corinthian church seemed to be in the "dog house"! This time it was over their behavior at the Lord's Supper. It was the custom that a community meal would include the ritual of the Lord's Supper. In just a few verses (11:17-34) Paul enumerated a list of transgressions committed by the members at the time of this meal. There were divisions in the church; when they assembled for the Lord's Supper, they started to eat without waiting for others; some people never got anything to eat and went away hungry; and some got drunk! Paul asked sarcastically, "Don't you have homes in which you can eat when hungry, and drink until you get drunk? What is your problem? Are you trying to show lack of respect for the church? Or are you trying to humiliate the poorer members of the congregation who have little food to share?" Paul concluded by suggesting that if they could not wait to eat until the proper time, they should eat before they left home!

8

1 Corinthians 12:4-27

Faith, Incorporated

LEARNING MENU

Based on what you know about your class members, their needs and the ways in which they learn best, choose at least one learning activity from each of the three Dimensions.

Opening Prayer
*As you cause the sun to rise, O God,
bring the light of Christ to dawn in our souls
and dispel all darkness.
Give us grace to reflect Christ's glory;
and let his love show in our deeds,
his peace shine in our words,
and his healing in our touch,
that all may give him praise, now and forever. Amen.*

(From *Book of Common Worship*, © 1993 Westminster/John Knox Press; page 500. Used by permission of Westminster/John Knox Press.)

Dimension 1: What Does the Bible Say?

(A) Answer Dimension 1 questions.

Answers to questions in the study book include the following:

1. While the spiritual gifts given to each may vary, yet they are given with the expectation that they will be used for the benefit of all (1 Corinthians 12:7).

2. The nine "manifestations of the spirit" mentioned by Paul are found in 1 Corinthians 12:8-10. They are:
—"wisdom" (2:6-16);
—"knowledge" (1:5; 8:1; 13:2, 8);
—"faith" (2:5; 16:13);
—"gifts of healing" (For healings attributed to Paul see Acts 14:8-10);
—"working of miracles" (1 Corinthians 12:28; Galatians 3:5);
—"prophecy" (13:2, 8; 14:1-5);
—"the discernment of spirits" (This may refer to the ability to distinguish between true and false prophecy. See 14:29);
—"various kinds of tongues (14:1-5);
—"interpretation of tongues" (14:26-28).

3. In 12:14-21 Paul enumerated various parts of the body and their relationship with each other. Note in verse 21 that the "head" is not given special honor, but is simply listed as one of the parts of the body.

4. In 12:23b Paul suggests that the "less respectable" members of the body should be treated with greater respect. The reference here is to the sexual organs, covered in many cultures to avoid shame. Here Paul uses this as an analogy, urging that members of the church with lower social and economic standing be respected and where appropriate, cared for by the church. (See page 68 in study book.)

(B) Understand nine spiritual gifts.

Before the activity:
- Write each of the spiritual gifts listed in activity (A), question 2, at the top of a separate sheet of paper, one gift to a sheet. On each sheet also include the Bible reference associated with that item. Do not post these sheets. They will be given to work groups in Step Two.
- Provide chalkboard or large sheets of paper.

During the session:
Step One:
- Ask all class members to find 12:8-10. The first step is simply to list the nine "manifestations of the spirit" as found in this passage. Ask class members to name them while you record them on chalkboard or a large sheet of paper.

Step Two:
- Divide the class into nine parts. Each part may consist of one or more persons.
- Give each group one of the pages prepared before class. (If there are fewer than nine persons present, divide the class into three parts, with three "gift" sheets for each part.)
- Instruct each group to read again 12:8-10, and to read the additional reference(s) related to the "gift" or "gifts" to which they were assigned.
- Invite groups to explain the meaning of their assigned "gift" to the rest of the class.
- Record any unanswered questions on the page provided.

Step Three:
- Using the order of the "gifts" as recorded in Step One, ask each group to report its findings. Allow time for discussion.

(C) Sing.

Before the activity:
- Invite an instrumentalist to accompany singing.
- Find hymnals containing the hymn "One Bread, One Body" (*The United Methodist Hymnal*, No. 620).

When the activity begins:
- Learn what may be a new hymn for your church. "One Bread, One Body" is based on Corinthians and Galatians, especially 1 Corinthians 12. Although a Communion hymn, it is appropriate to sing it whenever the church gathers as a community of faith.
- As the instrumentalist plays the melody, encourage class members to read the words of the first verse.
- Invite a good reader to read aloud 1 Corinthians 12:12-27.
- Sing all the stanzas of the hymn.

Dimension 2: What Does the Bible Mean?

(D) Identify another's gifts.

Before the activity:
- Provide one sheet of paper for each person and pencils for those who may need them. Say: "All people have been 'gifted' by God, but life experience for many people has underscored their inadequacies, not their gifts. This activity is intended to be an affirmation of the truth that we are all God's, that each one is a special person, and that all have been blessed with gifts that can be seen by others, if not by ourselves."

When the activity begins:
- Ask students to number off by four's.
- Ask students to stand and find a partner. Partners should consist of persons numbered one and three OR persons numbered two and four. (This system provides that persons will not be paired with a person sitting next to them. It also provides for friendly chatter before the serious discussion begins!) Ask pairs to sit together.
- Make a statement something like the following: "Paul believed that God gives each of us a gift, perhaps many gifts. Often it is easier for us to look at another person and say, 'How gifted!' than to acknowledge our own God-given gifts. Although Paul said that we should not think of ourselves more highly than we ought to think, he did not mean that we should deny our own strengths."
- Ask each person to write on a piece of paper the special gift or gifts they see that are possessed by the other person. (Tell them that at the close of this activity, they will be asked to give this paper to the one they have been describing.)
- Each person, in turn, will share what they have written. When both persons in the pair have shared, they will exchange their notes.
- Reassemble class and ask:
—How did it feel to be told positive things about yourself? (Paul's conclusion would be that since all people are gifted by God, all are equal in God's sight.)

(E) Experience diversity of physical abilities.

- Before the session, collect the following: material for blindfolds, ear plugs, heavy mittens, crutches, and a box of various small items such as a marble, a coin, a snapshot, a paper clip, and so forth. Provide one of these miscellaneous boxes for every ten class members.
- Using the materials collected, provide each person with a physical "diversity."
- Ask groups of ten to form in various parts of the room. Be sure that each group is diverse in its physical abilities. For example, don't put all "blind people" in one group.
- After they have formed their groups, place the box of small objects on the floor, in the center of each group.
- Give each person a piece of paper and a pencil.
- Invite each person to examine the objects in the box and write a description of the box contents.
- Watch, without comment, as each individual and each group tries to accomplish the task. (People with mittens won't be able to pick up the objects, blindfolded persons won't be able to see them, those with crutches will find it difficult to stoop to the floor, people with ear plugs may find it difficult to follow directions.)
—How will each group respond to this task?
- When most groups have completed the task, ask:
—What happened in your group?
—What does it mean to be the body of Christ? (27)

TEACHING TIP

One of the reasons for this activity is to help class members feel the deprivation experienced when all of their body parts are not functioning together. Equally as important, however, is understanding Paul's discourse about the body as an analogy of how the church as the body of Christ may be composed of various diversities, yet is called to work together in unity.

(F) Describe baptism.

Before the session:
- Provide extra Bibles.
- On chalkboard or a large sheet of paper write: "1 Corinthians 12:13; Colossians 3:10-11; and Galatians 3:27-28. (This activity is related to the sidebar in the study book, "A Baptismal Affirmation.")

When the activity begins:
- Ask class members to form groups of three.
- Instruct each group to locate and read one of the Bible references posted.
- Compare, and note the differences.
- Call the group together, and hear reports on findings.
- Refer to "A Baptismal Affirmation."

(G) Wonder. . . .

- Ask class members to find the paragraph in the study book that begins, "He [Paul] did not identify Christ as 'head' of the body" (page 66). Ask:
—What does this do to the argument stated like this: "As Christ is the head of the church, so is the husband the head of the wife." (No conclusions need to be drawn in this session. Perhaps there can be more discussion in session 12 when Ephesians is the focus.)

(H) Tell stories of community.

The members of Christ's body are described in the study book (page 66) as "existing for one another . . . serving and caring for one another . . . and sharing in one another's sufferings, honors, and joys."

- This is storytelling time. Help class members identify and talk about groups they have known about or of which they have been or are now a part, which fit the above description. They may tell about family groups, a church Sunday school class, a prayer group, people at their work place, an addiction support group, a professional group, an army barracks, or even a gang. Be prepared for surprises. While we might expect that many such groups are church related, this is hardly ever the case.
- This activity requires sympathetic listening, and appreciation for the willingness to share.
- Following the sharing of stories, ask:
—Is it possible for God's spirit to be present and God's love to be mediated through non-church groups?

Dimension 3: What Does the Bible Mean to Us?

(I) Plan for developing church leaders.

If your church is like many, willing workers may be recruited for whatever job is calling the loudest, with only minimal attention to the potential worker's greatest gifts. How can the church insure that people will be able to use their God-given gifts in their church-related volunteer tasks?

- Ask half of the class members to imagine that they comprise the church membership and evangelism committee. The task of this group is twofold: (1) to devise a way to help prospective members understand that, among other things, membership means participation in the work of the church; and (2) to help them visualize what this might mean for them. Where should this process begin?

- The other half of the class will imagine itself to be "The Gifts and Graces Committee" (perhaps a new committee in your church). The task of this group will be to devise a plan that will guarantee that all members of the church are working in the area of their greatest gifts and graces.
- After about fifteen minutes, reassemble the members and hear reports.
— Have any new ideas been generated that might work in your church? (If so, don't let them get lost.)
— What next steps might be taken?

TEACHING TIP

These groups may need your help to stay on the subject.

(J) Visualize your gifts in action.

The church, as an institution, needs volunteers who will offer their God-given gifts as church school teachers, ushers, choir members, treasurers, preparers of food, custodians, and countless other tasks that keep the church running smoothly. But people are needed who will take their gifts into the secular world also, and there put them to use for the glory of God. This, in the long run, may be the more difficult assignment.

- To begin the discussion of this question, ask:
— In your place of work, (home, office, factory, school, farm, science laboratory, and so forth), how can you put your gifts to work in the service of God?

TEACHING TIP

If activity (D) is chosen in Dimension 2, activity (J) may be used as a follow-up. In this case, you may want to return to the original partners for the discussion.

(K) Discover the meaning of "church."

Everyone knows that the church is a building and that it houses people who call themselves Christian. But what does it mean to the people inside the church? How are the lives of class members different because of this church or some other one? What would the world be like if there were no churches?

- Discuss:
— What replies have you received since last week when you completed the sentence, "The church for me is. . ."?
— What replies to this question did you receive from the "On the Street Interviewers" today as they questioned people on their way into the church?
— What is your response as class members to this question?
— What do all of these responses say about the church as "the body of Christ?"

(L) Name the work of the church in the world.

Before the session:
- Gather current newspapers from which headlines may be cut.
- Provide several pairs of scissors.
- Locate a copy of the social concerns statement for your church and/or denomination.

When the activity begins:
- Invite class members to cut out newspaper headlines that point to troubled people and troubled places on this planet. Gather these to use later during this activity. (It would probably be easy for people to list what they want the church to do for them personally, their families, and even the community. Harder is to describe what the church can do for the problems of the world.)
- Read aloud the headlines.
- Put them into stacks on the table according to general categories that emerge as you read. Categories might include the following: Violence, Poverty, War, Drugs, and so forth.
- Let the group choose one category. Reread those headlines and ask the question: What can the church do about these problems?
- Share relevant portions of the denomination's or local church's statement about social concerns.
— Is this one way that the church can "manifest God's grace in its corporate life"? (see the study book, page 68.)

(M) Write it down.

Continue to encourage members in the use of their notebooks. What unanswered questions are left at the completion of this session? What new insights have emerged that they intend to act upon?

Additional Bible Helps

The Collection for Jerusalem
Paul began his work among the Gentiles with the approval of the Jewish-Christian community in Jerusalem. Included in this agreement was the understanding that Paul would take a collection from his Gentile churches as an act of charity to benefit the poor in the church at Jerusalem. Galatians 2:10 notes the beginnings of this collection project. In 1 Corinthians 16:1-4 Paul explained the procedure to the church at Corinth:
— On the first day of every week Christians were asked to put away extra money from their earnings.
— When Paul arrived for a visit he would receive the money.

—The church would appoint people to take the money to Jerusalem. (This gesture on the part of Paul may have been to assure the Corinthians that he would not use the collection for his own needs.)
—Paul would provide a letter to go with the collections and might even accompany those officially appointed to make the trip to Jerusalem.

The Beginning of a Long Tradition
Little is known about the result of these offerings, other than that it may have been the beginning of a long tradition of church collections!

In one of Paul's letters to the church at Corinth he described how the churches of Macedonia, a poor region compared with the environs of Corinth, had given most generously. Apparently the church at Corinth had "pledged" but had yet to "pay their pledge"! He prodded a bit, using the Macedonians as a good example (chapter 9). Eventually they did make good their word, for in the letter to the church at Rome (Romans 15:25-27) Paul reported that both Macedonia and Achaia (the province of which Corinth was the capital) had given an offering. It was his expectation that after delivering the money to Jerusalem, he would be on his way to Rome. (Apparently, by the time Paul wrote the letter to the Romans, he had decided that he would, in fact, accompany those who had been appointed to take the money to the church at Jerusalem.)

The Thirteenth Chapter of First Corinthians
Known by many as "the love chapter," 1 Corinthians 13 may well be one of the best known chapters in the Bible. Without question, it is a literary masterpiece. There is some speculation that it may have been written separately, as a liturgical piece, and then inserted by Paul into this letter.

This chapter is placed within the context of a discussion of spiritual gifts. (See the sidebar on spiritual gifts in the study book, page 64.) Chapter 12 begins and ends with a discussion of gifts of the Spirit. The last verses of this chapter refer to speaking in tongues.

Chapter 13 insists that love is of more value than any of the spiritual gifts. In fact, others are temporary and will pass away, but love is permanent and will remain forever. When we come face to face with the Divine, the spiritual gifts are left behind, and it is God's own love that remains.

Chapter 14 returns to a discussion of spiritual gifts, paying special attention to the gifts of prophecy and speaking in tongues.

Glossolalia
Glossolalia is translated literally "speaking in tongues," which must have sounded like a foreign language to most who heard it. This experience seems to have been an important one for some of the early Christian communities. While Paul acknowledged that the ability to speak in tongues and to interpret was one of the spiritual gifts, he suggested to his readers that they "strive for the greater gifts" (1 Corinthians 12:31).

In chapter 14 Paul insisted that "tongues" not be a part of worship unless an interpreter is present. If the speaking cannot be understood, then it can neither instruct nor build up the believing community. Furthermore, unless able to be understood, the speaking makes an ineffective witness to unbelievers. Finally, Paul was not sure that speaking in tongues would help the church's reputation. "If, therefore, the whole church comes together and all speak in tongues, and outsiders or unbelievers enter, will they not say that you are out of your mind?" (NRSV) Nevertheless, in chapter 14 Paul provided some regulations for those times when speaking in tongues occurred:

—Tongues should be spoken only when there is someone present who can interpret what has been said.
—There should be no more than three persons speaking in tongues on any one occasion.
—Those speaking in tongues should take turns, not speak all at once.

These regulations were probably intended to aid in the building up of the church and providing a context of decency and order.

9
2 Corinthians 5:12–6:2

A New Creation

LEARNING MENU

Based on what you know about your class members, their needs and the ways in which they learn best, choose at least one learning activity from each of the three Dimensions.

Opening Prayer
Eternal God,
your touch makes this world holy.
Open our eyes to see your hand at work
in the splendor of creation,
and in the beauty of human life.
Help us to cherish the gifts that surround us,
to share your blessings with our sisters and brothers,
and to experience the joy of life in your presence.
We ask this through Christ our Lord. Amen.

(From *Book of Common Worship*, © 1993 Westminster/John Knox Press; page 500. Used by permission of Westminster/John Knox Press.)

Dimension 1: What Does the Bible Say?

(A) Answer Dimension 1 questions.

Answers to questions in the study book include the following:

1. Christ died for everyone so that everyone would be able to live for Christ, rather than for themselves (15; see also Romans 7:4 for a similar statement).

2. Now because of Christ's death and resurrection, all the old has passed away, and everything has been made new (16-17). This is reminiscent of Old Testament passages in Isaiah 43:18-19; 65:17; and 66:22.

3. Actions or functions that Paul attributed to Christ include the following:
— Christ's love urged on Paul and everyone (2 Corinthians 5:14);
— through Christ humankind is reconciled to God (18);
— through Christ the entire world is reconciled to God (19);
— humankind's trespasses will not be counted against them (19);

—through Christ we become "the righteousness of God" (21).

4. All persons need to be reconciled to God, and through Christ, God has taken the initiative.

(B) Compare Bible references to "new creation."

In using the phrase, "new creation," Paul remembered a concept from the Hebrew Scriptures. In what way, if any, did Paul add new meaning to this phrase?
- Divide the class into two groups (or more if the class is large).
- On chalkboard or a large sheet of paper write these four references: Isaiah 43:18-19; 65:17; 66:22; 2 Corinthians 5:16-17.
- Assign to each group one of these references. The groups' task is to describe the meaning of "new creation" as understood in these verses.
- Summarize by hearing reports in the order in which the references have been listed.
—How do they differ?
- Contrast Paul's meaning with that in the Isaiah passages. (For an extensive discussion of 2 Corinthians 5:16-17, see *II Corinthians: A New Translation with Introduction and Comments*, by Victor Paul Furnish, The Anchor Bible Series, Vol. 32A. Doubleday, 1984; pages 329-333.)

(C) Find another word for *atonement*.

In traditional Christian terminology, the concept "Christ died for our sins," is one theory of atonement. His death made it possible for humanity to be "at-one" with God. If activity (G) is chosen this activity may become a part of the closing discussion of that activity.
Before the session:
- Provide Bibles in three translations: Revised Standard Version, New Revised Standard Version, and King James Version.
- Ask early arrivals to find Romans 5:11 in each of the three versions.

When the activity begins:
- Invite early arrivals to respond to the following:
—How do these three versions differ?
—What word is used in the RSV and NRSV in place of the word *atonement*?

Dimension 2:
What Does the Bible Mean?

(D) Describe Paul's religious occupation.

We know that Paul's secular occupation was as a tentmaker. What was his occupational relationship to the Christian church?
Before the session:
- Secure several copies of Bible dictionaries, for example, *Harper's Bible Dictionary* or *Interpreter's Dictionary of the Bible*.
- Write on chalkboard or a large sheet of paper (leaving space for definitions) the following words: "Disciple," "Apostle," "Evangelist," "The Twelve."

When the activity begins:
- Invite participants to find definitions for these words in the references provided.
- Record significant responses on chalkboard or a large sheet of paper.
- Ask:
—How is each category defined?
—Which of these descriptions can be used to accurately describe Paul? Are you sure?

(E) Explore the meaning of *outsiders*.

In the study book discussion of Dimension 2, page 70, the "rival apostles" who came to Corinth were called "outsiders." This activity explores the meaning of *outsider* and asks: "Who is the outsider?"
- Use this optional warm-up exercise:
—Does your class remember the children's game, "Cat and Mouse," where the object was to keep the cat on the outside of the circle, away from the mouse who was in the inside of the circle? Play this game for a few minutes, but name the game "Outsiders and Insiders."
- Summarize the first five paragraphs of Dimension 2 in the study book, pages 70-71.
- Divide the class into groups of no more than eight persons.
- Designate half of the groups as members of the church at Corinth.
- Designate half of the groups as "rival apostles."
- The "Corinthian" groups and the "rival apostles" groups should move as far away from each other as the size of the room will allow.
- Provide sheets of paper and a marker for each group of eight or less. The task is to list reasons why each of the following statements is true:
—We are the "insiders."
—They are the "outsiders."

- Reassemble and hear the results.
- Discuss the reports. Ask:
—Is this a debate unique to the first century church?

(F) Create a metaphor for Paul.

By this ninth session of the unit, the class is well on its way to knowing Paul's character and personality. Jesus used a metaphor when he said that Peter was "like a rock" on which the church would be built. An energetic child might be said to be "like a bull in a china shop!" Or a stressed adult might be said to be "like a bomb waiting to explode."
- Consider:
—If Peter is "like a rock," what metaphors can your class create to describe Paul?
- Give each person a piece of paper and a pencil. Ask each to complete this sentence: "Paul is like. . . ."
- Hear the suggestions from the class. Choose the three metaphors class members think are most descriptive of Paul.
- Focus class discussion on this question: What does Christianity most need today? A Peter? Or a Paul?

(G) Fingerpaint the feeling of "reconciliation."

TEACHING TIP

Reconciliation is not only a concept to be learned, but an experience to be felt. Mind and heart together provide the basis for understanding. (This is a creative activity that includes several sub-activities as well as extensive discussion. It will require at least thirty minutes of class time.)

Before the session:
- Prepare the classroom for the fingerpainting activity. (See the sidebar, "Preparing to Fingerpaint," on page 19 of this leader's guide.)

When the activity begins:
- This activity has four steps. In Steps 1, 2, and 3 each person will work alone. Step 4 is a group summarizing discussion.

Step 1:
- Ask each person to silently recall an experience in which they felt estranged or alienated from someone they loved. Can they recall how they felt? Reassure them that they will not be asked to describe or identify this situation.
- Send participants to the fingerpainting area to "paint" the way they felt as a result of this estrangement. Allow five minutes for this step.
- Designate a corner of the room where finished pictures will be placed.

Step 2:
- Encourage each person to recall an experience of estrangement or alienation that was resolved in a positive way. (This need not be the experience recalled for Step 1.)
- Repeat the reassurance about privacy, as in Step 1.
- Allow about five minutes for this step.
- Designate a different corner of the room where finished pictures may be placed.

Step 3:
- Invite members to walk around the room, observing the paintings. This should be done in silence, to avoid the temptation to make value judgments about another's work.

Step 4:
- Reassemble for debriefing and discussion. Urge people to respond only to the specific question as asked. There are no wrong answers! Suggested questions:
—Briefly, as you explored the finished paintings, what did you observe?
—In your own work, which of the paintings did you find most difficult?
—Which did you most enjoy doing?
—What single word or short phrase best describes for you the first group of paintings that were made? (Write these on a large sheet of paper or chalkboard under the heading "Separation/Alienation.")
—What single word or short phrase best describes for you the second group of paintings? (Write these under the heading "Reconciliation.")
- Read 2 Corinthians 5:18-19. Relate estrangement and alienation from God and reconciliation with God, to the feelings evoked by the fingerpainting activity.
—Are there parallels?

(H) Offer a gift.

This activity underscores the fact that a gift offered is not really a gift until it has been received. (See the study book, Dimension 2, page 74.)
- With no explanation about this activity, ask for three volunteers to leave the room. Send with them a piece of paper on which is written: "You will be asked to return to the room, one person at a time. Each will be offered a "gift." The first two will refuse to receive the gift. Regardless of how much the class urges, they must not accept it! The third will accept it with appreciation." DO NOT reveal the contents of this message to class members who remain in the room!
- When volunteers have left, those who remain decide on an imaginary gift that will be offered to the volunteers when they return. It should be an attractive gift that anyone would be glad to receive. Do not choose money! Be imaginative!
- Ask volunteers to return, one at a time. Offer the gift to

each in turn. If they refuse it, let the class try to convince them.
• Discuss: The class generously offered a wonderful gift, but was powerless to force it upon those who refused.
—How did it feel to be refused?
• Relate this to God's offer of reconciliation to us.

Dimension 3: What Does the Bible Mean to Us?

"Reconciling love" is extended to humankind by God, and may also be extended by one person to another person. In Dimension 3 the author of the study book asks this question: "What is the character of the reconciling love that constitutes the gospel by and to which we are called?" (page 74)

Four specific characteristics are suggested. All of these characteristics are addressed in the activities of Dimension 3.

(I) Explore the meaning of "tough love."

The first characteristic of reconciling love is that it is constant and unconditional. Many times in life's relationships this kind of love is tested. How does one respond?
• Invite a family counselor to present the concept of "tough love" for class discussion.

(J) Struggle with the requirement to love everyone.

Before the session:
• Save current newspapers several days before class.

When the activity begins:
The second characteristic of reconciling love is that it is universal and inclusive. God's love is offered to all. So should ours be.
• Give each person present several pages from a current newspaper.
• Share that the task for each person is to find articles that feature a person or groups of people whom others might find difficult to love.
• Lead class members in sharing their findings.
• Discuss:
—Does God love these people?
—If human beings offered reconciling love to people described in the newspapers, what would it look like?

(K) Live for others; make a plan.

Before the session:
• Select several situations in your own community that illustrate injustice, oppression, economic exploitation, or natural disaster. Prepare to describe these briefly.
The third characteristic of reconciling love is that it frees us to live for others rather than for ourselves.

When the activity begins:
• Present the situations you have selected, and ask for clarification and brief discussion.
• Ask:
—How can this class show reconciling love in these situations?
• Let the group choose one on which they are willing to work.
• Make a plan. (The first step may be to develop a small task force that will (1) do further research, and (2) bring a specific plan to the next session.

(L) Compare concepts of "invitation" and "coercion."

The fourth characteristic of reconciling love is that it *invites* us but *does not coerce* us. An example of coercion might be illustrated by the following statement made by a parent to a disobedient child: "I love you, but you can't go out to play until you say 'I'm sorry.'" This is coercion.

On the other hand, if a parent says to a disobedient child, "I love you. When you feel sorry, I'll be here to listen." This is an invitation.
• Lead the class in thinking of other illustrations which contrast love that is invitational with love that coerces.
• Ask:
—Does God ever coerce?

(M) Share experiences when attitudes changed.

• We sometimes "wake up" to discover that old grudges and prejudices are no longer appropriate. Review the story of Sergeant Yokoi as told in the study book.
• Invite class members to share personal experiences. Do not coerce!

(N) Write it down.

• Encourage members to write reflections on this session as soon after the session as possible.

Additional Bible Helps

A Painful Incident: A Mystery
Reading the Bible is sometimes like reading a mystery story. Enough details are given to keep us glued to the text, searching for the bits and pieces that will reveal the identity of the villain. The reference in 2 Corinthians 2:5-11 is a case in point.

The mystery centers on an incident that has taken place, apparently within the Corinthian congregation. A man (we don't know who) had done something (we don't know what) to someone (we're not sure to whom) that had been brought to the attention of Paul (of this we are sure)!

Traditionally, the unnamed man has been assumed to be the "incestuous man" described in 1 Corinthians 5:1-5 and discussed in the Additional Bible Helps for Session 7. While little else is known about this man, it is fairly clear that he was a member of the Christian community at Corinth.

What had this man done that warranted such concern? Both the man and the offense seem to be so well known that Paul saw no reason to make further identification. Most likely false or malicious statements had been made about Paul in a way that had endangered his reputation. The accusations were probably made to Paul, face-to-face, during his last visit in Corinth.

But are we sure who has been so slandered by this unnamed member of the church? Paul went out of his way to indicate that the offense was not to himself, but his passion makes it reasonable to assume that he may have been the primary target of the accusations. Had it been an associate so slandered (as some suggest), Paul would undoubtedly have felt the slander just as personally. In fact, the burden of Paul's concern was that, because of this incident, the integrity of the entire congregation had been called into question. This concern is consistent with the principle he set forth in his earlier letter, using the human body and its parts as an analogy for the church: "If one member suffers, all suffer together with it; if one member is honored, all rejoice together with it" (1 Corinthians 12:26).

This was not the first time Paul had written to the Corinthian church about this incident. In 2:4-5 he referred to an earlier letter, written "with many tears." (This is now referred to as "the tearful letter.") While this letter has not been preserved, Paul may have suggested that some kind of disciplinary action should be taken.

When Paul wrote these words in 2 Corinthians 2:5-11, they were after the fact. The incident had occurred. The pain had been real. The offender had been disciplined (we don't know how) by action of the congregation. Paul wrote to say, "enough is enough." He pleaded that it was time for the congregation to effect a reconciliation with the one who created this incident and to reach out with forgiveness, consolation, and a reaffirmation of love.

Who Wrote 2 Corinthians 6:14–7:17?

The authorship of this passage is problematic. On the one hand, it appears in a letter known to have been written by Paul. On the other hand, it doesn't sound like Paul!
—It expresses an exclusive attitude that is not typical of Paul.
—Verse 7:1 does not square with Paul's emphasis on righteousness as a gift, as opposed to earning it through making ourselves holy.
—It is unclear why Paul would disrupt the flow of the argument to insert these verses that contain ideas drawn primarily from the Hebrew Scriptures, and that do not support the argument he is making.

If these verses are not an integral part of this Pauline letter, placed intentionally at this particular place, then what is their source, and why were they placed here? There is no end to the speculation.
—This may have its origin in the Qumran community of the first two centuries B.C., since there are numerous parallels between concepts in this passage and some in the Dead Sea Scrolls.
—One suggestion is that it may be a passage against Paul that reflects the ideas of his opponents.
—It may be a non-Pauline passage added by a later editor.
—It could be a fragment from the letter mentioned by Paul in 1 Corinthians 5:9.
—Perhaps this is material previously written by Paul or someone else, and inserted here by Paul to warn the Corinthians not to associate with his enemies.
—It has even been suggested that this passage may have been a deliberate attempt to get the attention of his readers by using uncharacteristic language.

For every speculation a counter argument can be found. Where these verses came from and why they are located at this place in the letter, remain as yet another mystery. Therefore, it is problematic to indicate anything from these verses as Paul's thought. At the very least, if cited, it should be done so tentatively!

10
2 Corinthians 11:21b–12:10

Strength Through Weakness

LEARNING MENU

Based on what you know about your class members, their needs and the ways in which they learn best, choose at least one learning activity from each of the three Dimensions.

Opening Prayer
Eternal God, you never fail to give us each day all that we ever need,
and even more. Give us such joy in living
and such peace in serving Christ,
that we may gratefully make use of all your blessings,
and joyfully seek our risen Lord
in everyone we meet.
In Jesus Christ we pray. Amen.

(From *Book of Common Worship*, © 1993 Westminster/John Knox Press; page 500. Used by permission of Westminster/John Knox Press.)

Dimension 1: What Does the Bible Say?

(A) Answer Dimension 1 questions.

Answers to questions in the study book include the following:

1. The long list of hardships Paul had to endure included: being imprisoned; flogged with lashes (five times); beaten with rods (three times); stoned; shipwrecked (three times); adrift at sea; forded rivers; attacked by bandits; danger from his own people; danger from Gentiles; dangers in cities; dangers in the wilderness; danger at sea; dangers from "false" brothers and sisters; sleepless nights; hunger; thirst; lack of food; cold; nakedness; pressure because of anxiety about the churches; frantic and precarious exit from Damascus by basket and through a window in the city wall (see Acts 9:23-25 for a different, secondhand version of this same incident); his "thorn in the flesh."

TEACHING TIP

If you plan to lead the class in activity (B), list these hardships on a large sheet of paper or chalkboard as the answers are given.

2. The governor of Damascus guarded the city in an effort to seize Paul as he attempted to leave; but friends put him into a basket, let him down through a window in the wall, and facilitated his escape.

3. Paul suggested that God gave him the "thorn in his flesh" in order to keep him from being too elated over the visions and revelations he had received (7b).

4. When Paul prayed that this "thorn" might be removed, the answer was *No*. By this answer Paul understood that God was telling him that God's grace was sufficient, and that because of this weakness, he would be stronger.

(B) Count your hardships.

Before the activity:
- Provide each person with a piece of paper and pencil.

When the activity begins:
Instead of the song, "Count Your Blessings, Name Them One by One," Paul's theme song might have been, "Count Your Hardships, Name Them Dozen by Dozen!" In activity (A), question 1, hardships are listed.
- Ask class members to think about the hardships they have endured in the last fifteen years.
- Give the class two minutes to list them on paper provided.
- Compare their lists with Paul's list.
- Ask the class to find 2 Corinthians 12:9-10. Ask someone to read it aloud.
- Discuss:
—What does it mean for "power to be made perfect in weakness"?

Dimension 2: What Does the Bible Mean?

(C) Define *parody*.

Before the session:
- Collect several dictionaries and at least one thesaurus.

When the activity begins:
- As people arrive ask them to be ready to tell the class the meaning of *parody* as they find it in dictionaries and a thesaurus. (Chapter 11:1–12:13, known as a "fool's speech," cannot be properly understood except as a parody.
- Hear reports from class members on the meaning of *parody*.
- During reports, write key words on chalkboard or a large sheet of paper.
- Direct class members to find this "fool's speech" in their Bibles. They should read it silently, noting ways in which this is a parody.
- Discuss the class findings.

(D) Compare two accounts of the Damascus wall escape.

Before the session, prepare a wall chart, following the pattern of "Paul's Escape From Damascus" (see Additional Bible Helps for this session, page 52.) However, enter only the Bible references in the vertical lines; enter only the categories in the first horizontal column. This is a brief exercise that can be done as a total group.
- Divide the class in half, either by numbering off by two's, by indicating alternate rows, or dividing down the middle of the room. For this activity they will not physically move into these groupings.
- One half of the class will read Acts 9:22-29; the other half will read 2 Corinthians 11:30-33.
- Ask members to complete the chart. Do not share the "answers" in the leader's guide unless people are having difficulty discovering the answers.
- Discuss the results.
—Why is Acts so much more specific, when 2 Corinthians is a firsthand account?

(E) Talk about "religious experience."

- Divide into groups of two or three persons.
- Encourage persons to share with each other their own understanding of what is meant by "religious experience."
- As a total group, hear any comments members wish to make. One's personal religious experience can be known only by the one who experienced it. Therefore, insist that comments be accepted and not open for argument.
- Discuss Paul's account of his own religious experience as told in 2 Corinthians 12:2-5. The writer of the study book says, "As it turns out, there is very little to tell about it."
- Read another report of religious experience as written in Acts 22:6-11.
- Speculate with the class:
—If this happened to Paul as reported in Acts, why did he not cite this experience?

(F) Wonder together about God's will.

Whatever the nature of Paul's "thorn in the flesh," one might ask three questions:
—Was this affliction intentionally given to Paul to enhance his ministry?
—Was the affliction, present without God's intention, a way for Paul to make a point?
—Could a compassionate God ultimately intend for us to suffer?

STRENGTH THROUGH WEAKNESS

- Introduce Weatherhead's three categories of God's will: *intentional*, *circumstantial*, and *ultimate*. (See the sidebar, "The Will of God.")

> **The Will of God**
>
> During World War II Leslie D. Weatherhead wrote a little book called *The Will of God* (Abingdon, 1944). Using the crucifixion of Jesus as illustration, he described three ways to talk about the will of God.
> 1. The *intentional* will of God was not that Jesus should be crucified, but that he should be followed.
> 2. The *circumstantial* will of God, God's will in the circumstances that [humanity's] evil provided, was that Jesus should accept death, but accept it in such a positive and creative way as to lead to:
> 3. God's *ultimate* will—namely, the redemption of [humanity]. . . .

Dimension 3: What Does the Bible Mean to Us?

(G) Research the meaning of *ministry*.

Before the session:
- Using a concordance, find all of the references for *minister* or *ministry* that are included.
- Write each reference (for example, "2 Corinthians 3:6") on a separate slip of paper.
- Provide dictionaries and a thesaurus.
  The purpose of this activity is to highlight the understanding that the words *minister* and *ministry*, while including clergy, are not limited to clergy. All Christians are called to be "ministers."

When the activity begins:
- Let each person select one reference, sight unseen, which they will locate in their Bible.
- A few members should be asked to check dictionary and thesaurus definitions.
- Hear what members have discovered. Record key words.
- Consider following this activity with either (H), (J), (K), or (L).

> **TEACHING TIP**
>
> The study book suggests that there are four distinguishing marks of an authentically Christian ministry, whether that be the ministry of an individual Christian, an ordained clergyperson, or the church as an institution of society. Activities (H) through (L) focus on these marks.

(H) Identify risks we are willing to take.

One mark of authentic Christian ministry is willingness to work hard and take risks.
- Read this situation to the class: You have been kidnapped by creatures from outer space. They ask, "Are you a Christian?" Before you have time to answer, they give you an option. They say, "If you say 'No,' you are free to leave. But in this box *(show the box)* are possible risks that you will be forced to take if you say 'Yes.' While blindfolded you will reach into the box and choose your risk. Whatever the risk, once you have taken it, you will be free to go. . . if you are able!"
- Engage the class in discussion:
—What kinds of risks might be in the box?
—How will you decide whether to say yes or no?
—Can you bargain, for instance, by indicating that you would say yes if assured that certain risks were not in the box?
—What kinds of risks are you willing to take?

(I) List risky issues for your church.

Willingness to take risks is one of the marks of an authentic Christian ministry.
- Lead the class in listing current social issues on which they think it would be risky for your church to take a stand. Although the church's particular position on each issue is not the focus of this activity, the activity may nevertheless generate heated discussion.
- Ask: Regardless of the position taken by the church, what consequences should the church be willing to accept in order to stand up for its principles, whatever they are? Some possible risks might be
—alienation and possible loss of church members;
—alienation of the church from other churches in the community;
—damage to the pastor's chance for future advancement;
—ridicule;
—destruction of church property;
—harassing phone calls to church members;
—embarrassment for children of the church;
—loss of church income;
—need to eliminate some church programs;
—physical harm to church leaders.

(J) Identify the "weak."

An authentic ministry identifies the weak, stands with them personally, and seeks to address the systemic, social issues that keep them from being fully-functioning human beings.
- Ask the class to respond:
—Who are the weak with whom we should stand?
- List responses on chalkboard or a large sheet of paper.

- Help the group choose one of these categories of people on which the class will focus.
- Divide into three groups.
- Assign discussion topics:
—Group 1: What can we as individual Christians do to address this need?
—Group 2: What can this church do to address the immediate needs of these people?
—Group 3: What could this church, or this denomination, do to address the root causes of these person's needs?

> **A Hard Truth**
> We cannot escape the fact that we are part of the world community. When some are weak, we all lose strength. "No man is an island. . . every man's death diminishes me . . . never send to know for whom the bell tolls; it tolls for thee." (John Donne, *Devotions*, 1623)

- Reassemble the group and hear reports from groups. Be alert for the possibility that there may be interest in forming a task group to work on this issue.
- Share "A Hard Truth."

(K) Choose a hymn.

- Arrange to have an accompanist for hymns.
- Collect hymnals that contain at least one hymn in each of the three groupings below:
—Group 1. "The Old Rugged Cross," (*The United Methodist Hymnal*, No. 504); "Alas! and Did My Savior Bleed," (No. 359); "Must Jesus Bear the Cross Alone?" (No. 424).
—Group 2. "In the Cross of Christ I Glory," (No. 295); "Jesus, Keep Me Near the Cross," (No. 301).
—Group 3. "God of the Sparrow, God of the Whale," (No. 122); "Morning Glory, Starlit Sky," (No. 194); "Sing, My Tongue, the Glorious Battle," (No. 296).
An authentic Christian ministry is committed to preaching the word of the cross. Many modern, turn-of-the-century Christians are uncomfortable with the cross as a symbol of faith.
- Read aloud a hymn from Group 1. If there are enough hymnals available, ask the class to follow as you read.
- Encourage class members to share what phrases held special significance or brought forth questions or troublesome concepts for them.
- Write the title of the hymn on a large piece of paper; then record comments under the title of each hymn.
- Repeat this process for hymns from Groups 2 and 3.
- Summarize by asking the class to decide which hymn best conveys their own understanding of the meaning of the cross.
- Sing a selected hymn.

(L) Write a statement about "grace."

An authentic Christian ministry speaks to the world of the cross as a word of grace.
- Divide the class into groups of three or four persons.
- For the sake of this activity, the name of this church is Grace Church. (Maybe it is!)
- The task of this group is the following:
Your church is developing a brochure for use in an upcoming evangelism program. The purpose of the brochure is to convey to prospective new members something of the spirit and life of Grace Church. Your task is to write a paragraph explaining how the church got its name.
- Class members may: (1) refer to the discussion of the fourth mark of authentic Christian ministry in the study book; (2) look at hymns in the hymnal under the topic "Grace"; (3) consult the "grace" reference in *Harper's Bible Dictionary* (HarperCollins, 1985); (4) look up "grace" in a standard dictionary and/or thesaurus.
- Regroup and hear results of this task.
- If your church really is Grace Church, share what you know of the naming process.

(M) Write it down.

This session concludes six sessions during which letters from Paul to the church at Corinth have been studied. As a summary activity, suggest reviewing the same questions found in session 4, activity (L).

Additional Bible Helps

Paul's "Thorn in the Flesh"
The nature of Paul's "thorn in the flesh" has been an intriguing question for many centuries. Paul made brief reference to it in the context of what has come to be known as "A Fool's Speech" (2 Corinthians 11:1–12:13). In a show of disdain for his rivals in Corinth, Paul mimicked what he perceived to be their excessive boasting. Then, in 12:7, he suggested that the "thorn" had been given to him so that he would not think himself above other people because of the things revealed to him by God.

Speculation as to the nature of the "thorn in the flesh" can be divided into three major categories.

1. *Physical or mental illness.* There have been many hunches expressed, but with no clear evidence, they remain only hunches. Some have suggested that he had severe headaches, perhaps migraines. Others have wondered if it might have been recurring fevers from malaria, a speech impediment, inflammation of the retina from long exposure to the sun, or perhaps epilepsy. Still others suggest a psychosomatic illness, perhaps hysteria or depression.

2. Persecution. Paul often wrote about the persecution that he faced in the form of physical abuse and imprisonment. Constantly living with the possibility of this kind of persecution would have been stressful. Perhaps even more hurtful was the emotional abuse he must have felt when he was ridiculed or opposed by his enemies, and misunderstood by his friends. Physical abuse and opposition from his adversaries may have been the "thorn" Paul prayed to have removed.

3. Spiritual trials. Even though Paul focused on the welfare of the church, in his letters he often revealed misgivings about himself. His "thorn" may have been his own personal anxiety, his experiences of spiritual torment or sexual temptations. Some suggest that his "thorn" may simply have been a profound sense of unworthiness.

After an examination of the options, there is still no way to identify with confidence the nature of Paul's "thorn in the flesh." Although it is more likely to have been physical or mental illness, or persecution, than spiritual trials, no option can be eliminated.

Is there anything we can say with certainty? The "thorn" was a constant presence, not something that seemed to come and go. Paul believed that it was present for a reason. He personalized this condition by referring to it as "a messenger of Satan," Satan often being understood as an agent of God's purposes.

Whatever it was, and although perhaps a constant aggravation, it was not such that it kept him from living a rigorous and vigorous life.

Paul's Escape From Damascus

Paul's escape by basket over the Damascus wall is noted in both Acts 9:22-25 and 2 Corinthians 11:30-33. The means of escape, the escapee, and the city from which the escape took place, are the same in both accounts. But here the similarity ends.

Scripture Reference	ACTS 9:22-25	2 CORINTHIANS 11:30-33
Paul's Condition	Powerful (22)	Weak (30)
Plot	Discovered by Paul (24)	No mention
Plotters	Jews (23)	Governor, under King Aretas (32)
Purpose of Plot	To kill Paul (23)	To seize (arrest) Paul (32)
Escape	Aided by disciples (25)	"Was let down" (no mention of who "let him down.")

It seems clear that the purpose for telling the story was quite different in each case. In Acts, more attention was given to the seriousness of the threat, while in his letter to the people in Corinth, Paul seemed more interested in the escape itself. The writer of Acts, recording the event 25-35 years after Paul's own telling, narrated this story in the context of a description of Paul as "powerful." Paul himself, however, used it to illustrate his weakness and vulnerability.

11

Children of Promise

Galatians 3:23–4:11

LEARNING MENU

On the basis of what you know about your class members, their needs and the ways in which they learn best, choose at least one learning activity from each of the three Dimensions.

Opening Prayer
O God,
you are the well-spring of life.
Pour into our hearts the living water of your grace,
that we may be refreshed to live this day in joy,
confident of your presence
and empowered by your peace,
in Jesus Christ our Lord. Amen.

(From *Book of Common Worship*, © 1993 Westminster/John Knox Press; page 501. Used by permission of Westminster/John Knox Press.)

Dimension 1: What Does the Bible Say?

(A) Answer Dimension 1 questions.

Answers to questions in the study book include the following:

1. Before the Galatians became Christian they were enslaved to three masters: law (3:23; 4:5); "elemental spirits of the world" (4:3, 9); and pagan gods (4:8).

2. The purpose of redemption, as stated in 4:5, is so that humanity might receive adoption as children of God. When people receive the spirit of Christ, they are no longer slaves, but become children, and as children, heirs of God.

3. In baptism all become one in Christ; and also become heirs of Abraham and are blessed by him (3:6-9, 27-29).

4. Paul's special concern about the Galatians was that they would return to the time when they were enslaved by beings who were not of God. If this happened, his work with them would have been in vain.

(B) Find Galatia.

In this unit all letters traditionally attributed to Paul, with one exception, carry the name of a town or city: Rome, Corinth, Ephesus, and Philippi. Some class members may assume that Galatia was a city also. Here is an opportunity for a mini-lecture!

- Post a map that traces the journeys of Paul. (See the *Bible Teacher Kit*, Abingdon, 1994.)
- Use the information from the section entitled, "The Region of Galatia," as material for this mini-lecture. (You will find it in Additional Bible Helps at the end of this session, pages 56-57.)

Dimension 2: What Does the Bible Mean?

(C) Sing a hymn.

- This session emphasizes that oneness in Christ breaks down any existing national, social, and gender barriers. The hymn, "In Christ There Is No East or West" (*The United Methodist Hymnal*, No. 548), is appropriate. The original text was written in 1913. In 1987 a new stanza was added, specifically based on Galatians 3:28.
- If your hymnal does not include this verse (below), you can line it out as it is sung. (Quickly read the next line as the singers come to the end of the preceding line.)

> *In Christ is neither Jew nor Greek,*
> *and neither slave nor free;*
> *both male and female heirs are made,*
> *and all are kin to me.*

(Laurence Hull Stookey, Copyright © 1987, The United Methodist Publishing House.)

- Consider:
—What is the meaning of the last line? With whom are we kin?
—What does it mean to be "kin"?

Freedom From "the Law"

What is "the law"? Specific meanings of "the law" in first century Christianity are unclear. Various understandings appear in scholarly literature: (1) the entire Old Testament; (2) the Mosaic law; (3) the totality of God's revelation, sometimes written, but other times found only in oral tradition; (4) the first five book of the Old Testament (the Pentateuch); (5) specific instructions regarding behavior (works of the law), for example, circumcision, dietary codes, distinctions between clean and unclean, and observance of certain special days and seasons.

What Paul Did Not Mean by "Freedom From the Law"

Paul was not suggesting that people of faith should, as a matter of principle, disregard all of the commandments in the law of Moses or society's moral and regulatory laws.

What Paul Did Mean by "Freedom from the Law"

Paul wanted to make it clear that keeping the law, was not the way to salvation.

(D) Explore the meaning of Galatians 3:28.

The study book suggests that people are identified mainly with reference to their race, ethnic origin, cultural heritage, gender, and social status.

- List these "identifications" on chalkboard or a large sheet of paper. Then ask:
—What other ways are people identified? Add to the list.
- Give people permission to brainstorm without judging whether their answers are "right" or "wrong." For this activity it is all right if some items mentioned might properly belong under one of the categories already on the list. Items added, for example, may include occupation, age, physical ability, educational achievement, sexual orientation, church affiliation, family configuration, or political party affiliation.
- Read Galatians 3:28 to the class. Paul understood that those within the community of faith represent diversity but that these differences no longer alienate one from the other. We are all "one in Christ Jesus."
- Follow this activity with activity (L) if you wish.

(E) Think about what Paul did *not* say.

> **TEACHING TIP**
> The purpose of this activity is to underscore the validity of raising questions about traditional beliefs. There is no conclusive or "right" answer to the question asked in this activity.

Before the session:

- Post a large sheet of paper on which the following has been written: Read Matthew 1:18. Then ask:
—When was Matthew written?
- Find reference to the birth of Jesus in Mark. Ask:
—When was Mark written?
- Read Luke 1:26-27. Then ask:
—When was Luke written?
- Find references to the virgin birth of Jesus in Paul's letters.
—When were Paul's letters written?

When the activity begins:

- Encourage students to work together to find the answers to the questions on the large sheet of paper. Bible dictionaries, concordances, and Bible commentaries will all be helpful. (See especially *HarperCollins Study Bible*, 1993; *Harper's Bible Dictionary*, 1985; and *Harper's Bible Commentary*, 1988.)
- As group members discover answers, write them on the paper.
- In Galatians 4:4-5 Paul reported that Jesus was born "of a woman." The study book notes that nowhere did Paul mention the virgin birth of Jesus. Ask:
—Why do you think Paul did not mention the virgin birth?

- Let the class suggest answers. Some might include the following: (1) Paul had never been told; (2) if he had been told, it wasn't important to him; (3) he knew, but forgot to mention it; (4) it was a faith statement affirmed by a later generation of Christians.
- Whatever else may be said, it is clear that the manner of Jesus' conception and birth was not a pivotal point in the theology of Paul.

(F) Research the meaning of "the law."

Before the session:
- Review references to "law" in a concordance.
- Select references from Romans, 1 and 2 Corinthians, Galatians, Ephesians, and Philippians—as many as you have class members.
- Write each on a separate slip of paper and place them in a box.

When the activity begins:
- Invite each class member to draw one reference from the box, find the reference, and silently read it.
- From their research, let class members report their own understanding of "the law."
- Refer the class to the study book, page 88, paragraph beginning, "Then why was the law given at all?"
- Ask: What three points did Paul make with reference to "the law"?

Dimension 3:
What Does the Bible Mean to Us?

Bearing the Cross in Freedom

Paul understood freedom not as the opportunity to pursue one's own interests but to be even more at the service of others. That this is costly service can be seen in the fact that in this charter of Christian freedom he also refers frequently to the cross. . . . This ideal of service and even self-sacrifice poses definite problems for women of all generations and nearly all cultures, who are socially educated to expect that their true happiness lies in service to others, while men are brought up to pursue their own goals.

But Paul may have done something quite radical here: he held up traditionally feminine values as ideals for everyone, male and female, and perhaps especially for the Christian men who were his principal addressees . . . Women too need to appropriate these values, but they need also to balance this ideal carefully against their legitimate psychological needs. Bearing the cross in freedom does not mean enduring abuse and victimhood, but living genuinely for others out of one's own inner freedom by claiming the inheritance of the "sons of God."

(*The Women's Bible Commentary*, from the chapter "Galatians," by Carolyn Osiek; Westminster/John Knox Press; pages 336-337)

(G) Discover Paul's concept of "freedom."

This activity addresses what appear to be Paul's paradoxical statements about freedom and slavery.
- Class members should number off by two's.
- Instruct all number one's to read Galatians 5:1; number two's, Galatians 5:13.
- Form partners consisting of one person from group 1 and one person from group 2.
- Discuss with partners the following:
—What is Paul's message to us about freedom?
- Debrief this exercise. Ask:
—Did women and men hear the message in the same way?
- Read aloud to the class one biblical scholar's discussion of these two verses. See the sidebar, "Bearing the Cross in Freedom." Allow time for further response.

(H) Compare statements of faith.

Before the session:
- Ask your pastor for your church's or denomination's statement of faith. Look in a hymnal where you may find several such statements.
—Does your local church include a creed, a statement or affirmation of faith, in the worship liturgy each week?
- Gather enough hymnals, church bulletins and available denominational formulations for use by each class member.
- Individuals may rarely articulate their personal statements of faith, although each week as part of a church's worship they may corporately read a creed or statement provided by the church.

When the activity begins:
- Ask each class member to list on a sheet of paper the basic religious beliefs they hold and by which they intend to live.
- Distribute statements of faith that have been assembled.
- Let members search these statements to find parallels to the ones they have written individually.
—Did members list any beliefs not included in published statements?
—Are there ideas in published faith statements with which class members cannot agree?
- The study book suggests that requiring adherence to a particular set of beliefs poses two problems. Summarize these problems.
- Elicit responses from the class.

(I) Write a cinquain.

- See session 2, activity (E) for directions.
- Share the statement from the study book: "Christian baptism is always 'into' a community of believers."

- Designate half of the group to use *one* as the first word of the cinquain, and the other half, the word *community*. Allow a brief time for individuals to write a cinquain.
- Ask for volunteers to read aloud their cinquains. Alternate reading cinquains with first lines that begin with the word *one* and first lines that begin with the word *community*.
- Ask the following questions:
— Does the first line of the poem make a difference in the mood and meaning? In what way?
— If Christian baptism is "always 'into' a community of believers," what does this say about the place of baptism in the life of a Christian?

(J) Create a faith journey statement—without words.

Before the activity:
- Provide construction paper in an assortment of colors. Plan to have at least twice as many sheets as the number of class members you expect to be present.

When the activity begins:
- Introduce this activity by saying in your own words: "Faith development is an ongoing process. Each experience of our life, from birth to death, contributes to its formation."
- Allow no more than four minutes for people to think in silence about their own journey of faith.
- After this time has elapsed, explain that they will now have four minutes to describe their own faith development—but without using words! By what journey have they arrived at the faith they affirm today?

Step One:
Class members will choose a piece of construction paper in a color that is consistent with their faith journey, if possible.
Step Two:
They will tear the paper in any way they wish to express their faith journey.
Step Three:
They will move around the room, enjoying without comment the creativity of others. Allow two or three minutes.
Step Four:
They will share their creativity with one other person, this time using words. Allow one minute for each person.

- Reassemble the group. Debrief the exercise. You may ask the following questions to stimulate sharing:
— How did it feel to participate in this activity?
— Was there any significance in the color construction paper you chose?
— Did you discover anything about yourself and your own faith journey that you had not realized before?
— What does the phrase *faith journey* mean to you now?

(K) Celebrate diversity.

This activity can follow activity (D) or it can stand alone.

Before the session:
- Secure a supply of balloons in a variety of shapes and sizes.
- Provide felt-tip markers in a variety of colors.

When the activity begins:
- Read aloud to the class Galatians 3:28. This activity is a celebration of the truth in this verse.
- Let each person choose a balloon, inflate it (some may need help), and write on it one of the ways by which people are identified. (If this is a follow-up of activity (D), class members will be able to choose from the list already posted.)
- On each balloon write Galatians 3:28.
- Decorate the classroom with the balloons in a way that says, *We are many, but we are one in Christ*. Consider making a banner with these words and placing it in a prominent place in the room. Doing so will provide a message for those who pass by the room. Other church members, out of curiosity, may investigate the reason for balloons in an adult Sunday school classroom.

(L) Plan to be an "agent of God's love."

The call to persons to act as "agents of God's love" is a recurring theme in Paul's letters. If your class did not experience activity (G) in session 5 in the context of 1 Corinthians, consider including it in this study of the Letter to the Galatians.

Additional Bible Helps

The Region of Galatia
It is difficult to know the exact geographical location or specific people to whom this letter was addressed. Galatia was not a town but a region. In Paul's day it was used in two different ways. *Galatia* might refer (1) to a geographical region in the north central part of Asia Minor or (2) to a Roman province that included the Galatian region, but also additional territory to the south.

This southern region included the towns of Iconium, Lystra, and Derby, and churches in these places were founded by Paul (Acts 14:1-23). This knowledge has given rise to the "south Galatia" theory.

Most scholars, however, hold to a "north Galatia" theory. The author of Acts did not seem to think of Iconium, Lystra, and Derbe as "Galatian" towns. When the writer of Acts did refer to "Galatia" (Acts 16:6; see also Acts 18:23), it is likely that the reference was to the northern part of the region.

Also at issue in this determination is the historic reliability of the Book of Acts. Since there seems to be no internal evidence in the Galatian letter itself identifying the specific location of the expected recipients, this may be a puzzle that has no solution.

The Letter

The earliest existing, written account of the initial period of Christian church history is found in the opening two chapters of Galatians. Here is the first complete statement that describes Gentile Christianity as a religious movement apart from Judaism. This letter to the churches in the region of Galatia was perhaps written in the mid A.D. 50's. It is an urgent, and sometimes bitter, letter in which Paul responded to reports that the Galatian churches had been influenced by "false teaching."

In the early verses of this letter Paul greeted the churches and then immediately spoke his mind: "As we have said before, so now I repeat, if anyone proclaims to you a gospel contrary to what you received, let that one be accursed!" (Galatians 1:9)

Who were these "accursed" whose messages and influence must now be countered by Paul? Were they "Judaizers," Jewish Christians who insisted that Gentile Christians conform to certain Jewish laws, especially circumcision and food laws? Or were they Jewish-Christian "gnostics," who interpreted certain Jewish law and customs in "mystical" ways? While these are the two main options, scholars do not find in the sources enough definite evidence to support either choice. Whoever the "false teachers," Paul wanted to assure his readers that his own teachings were the true ones, not received from another human being, but received "through a revelation of Jesus Christ" (Galatians 1:12).

Among other things that Paul was saying to this probably diverse group was that the gospel they had received through him was all they needed for salvation. He pleaded with them not to be taken in by those who suggested that circumcision was necessary for salvation.

Leaders in the Jerusalem Church

Paul spent very little time in Jerusalem, and when there his primary association was with Cephas (Peter), and to a lesser extent, with James. This personal contact with these leaders was significant, however, since Paul carried out his mission to the Gentiles with the support of the Jewish Christians in Jerusalem.

Paul, in general, sought to act as an independent preacher of the gospel, along with associates chosen by him. A few scholars, however, believe that he was actually subject to the authority of the leaders in the Jerusalem church. Chapter 2 records an account of one visit to Jerusalem and a controversy he had with Peter about the way the Jerusalem leaders were dealing with the issue of circumcision.

Simon/Peter/Cephas

Simon, a disciple called by Jesus, was nicknamed "Peter," from the Greek word for "rock." He was also known as "Cephas," from an Aramaic word, also meaning "rock." According to Matthew, Jesus said of him, "On this rock will I build my church." The stalwart, loyal, and impetuous character of this man is well known and documented in the gospels and the Book of Acts. It is only in Paul's letter to the Corinthians (1 Corinthians 15:3-5) that we learn that the first post-Resurrection appearance of Jesus was to Cephas (Peter).

As one of the leaders in the Jerusalem church, his mission was to the Jews (some think to those outside of Jerusalem), although references in Acts indicate that Cephas (Peter) may also have been responsible for converting Gentiles. He probably supported the compromise that was struck, allowing Gentile Christians to become accepted members of the Christian community.

Both tradition and textual evidence point to the probability that Cephas (Peter) died a martyr's death in Rome.

James

James is identified as the brother of Jesus, although the exact nature of this relationship has been debated. There are many options. He may have been a literal brother, or a half-brother, or perhaps a stepbrother. He could also have been a cousin, an associate, or a close friend. One of Jesus' post-Resurrection appearances was to James. Although not a follower during Jesus' lifetime, he joined with the Twelve and others after the Resurrection and Ascension.

About James' relationship to the church at Jerusalem there is also much speculation. He may have emerged, eventually, as the successor to Peter, who was the acknowledged leader of the church, although there is no real evidence to support this possibility. His mission was to the Jews and may have been limited to those in the city of Jerusalem itself, although once again, there is no hard evidence to support this idea. According to tradition, he was put to death by priestly authorities in Jerusalem a few years before the destruction of the Temple in A.D. 70.

12
One New Humanity
Ephesians 2:1-22

LEARNING MENU

On the basis of what you know about your class members, their needs, and the ways in which they learn best, choose at least one learning activity from each of the three Dimensions.

Opening Prayer
Eternal God,
you call us to ventures of which we cannot see the ending,
by paths as yet untrodden,
through perils unknown.
Give us faith to go out with courage,
not knowing where we go,
but only that your hand is leading us
and your love supporting us;
through Jesus Christ our Lord. Amen.

(From *Book of Common Worship*, © 1993 Westminster/John Knox Press; page 501. Used by permission of Westminster/John Knox Press.)

Dimension 1: What Does the Bible Say?

(A) Answer questions from the study book.

This activity can be combined with activity (C). Answers to the questions in the study book include the following:

1. According to Ephesians 2:10, God intends for human beings to engage in good works.

2. The Jews and the Gentiles were divided by a wall of hostility that was broken down by the death of Jesus on the cross.

3. Christ is identified in verse 14 as "our peace" and in verse 17, as a proclaimer of peace to those both near and far.

4. The foundation of God's household is the apostles and the prophets (2:20); the cornerstone [or "keystone"] is Christ Jesus (2:20); and this foundation becomes a holy temple, where God dwells (2:21).

(B) Find differences in Ephesians 1:1.

Before the session:
• Collect many different translations or versions of the New Testament. Be sure to include the Revised Standard Version and the New Revised Standard Version.

Others might include, *The Bible: An American Translation, The New English Bible, The New Testament in Modern English,* and *Good News for Modern Man.* Also provide at least one copy of *Harper's Bible Commentary,* and at least one copy of *The Interpreter's One-Volume Commentary on the Bible.*

TEACHING TIP

Although traditionally attributed to Paul, Pauline authorship of Ephesians is questioned by many biblical scholars. This activity provides a way to introduce this concept.

When the activity begins:
- Distribute the Bibles and commentaries.
- Ask each class member to find Ephesians 1:1, either the text itself or the commentary reference.
- Let various individuals read aloud Ephesians 1:1 from their Bibles while the class listens. Be sure that the RSV and NRSV references are read.
- Talk about what was read.
—How do the versions differ? (Some mention Ephesus as the destination for the letter and others do not.)
- Ask for a report from those who have read the commentaries.
—What do they say about the inclusion (or exclusion) of Ephesus from this passage?
- Ask those with RSV or NRSV versions to read the footnote for this verse. Hear their reports.
- Conclude this activity with more information about the Letter to the Ephesians. (See both the study book and "The Letter" in Additional Bible Helps for this session.)

Dimension 2: What Does the Bible Mean?

(C) Demolish a wall.

TEACHING TIP

If this activity is selected it should be the first activity of the session. It includes activity (A). The purpose of this activity is to help the class experience how it feels to be walled off from other human beings, as well as the joy of reunion.

Before the session:
- Erect a "wall" at least six feet high down the center of the classroom, creating an actual physical barrier. Use anything available, including chairs, tables, piano, cardboard boxes, chalkboard, coat racks, and your imagination! The denser the barrier, the better. The wall should be completed before the first class member arrives.
- Set up the room with chairs arranged on each side of the wall as in a classroom.
- Enlist a helper.

When the activity begins:
- As people enter, randomly assign them to one of the sides of this wall.
- Teach activity (A) simultaneously on each side of the wall. (The helper you recruited will lead one side, you will lead the other.)
- At a prearranged time, each leader should say to her or his group: "There is still another question to be answered. What are we going to do about this wall that separates us from the rest of the class?" (The expectation is that they will want to take it down, although the leader should be prepared for a maverick or two!)
- When the wall has been removed and order restored, assemble as a total group.
- Talk about how it felt to be separated.
- Read aloud Ephesians 2:11-22, which described the wall between Gentiles and Jews as a "wall of hostility."
—What other walls divide us from one another?
—How can these walls be broken down?

(D) Study a hymn.

Before the session:
- Provide hymnals containing "Let Us Plead for Faith Alone" (*The United Methodist Hymnal*, No. 385). If enough hymnals are not available for class use, write each stanza on a separate sheet of newsprint.
- This hymn was written by Charles Wesley in 1740 and is based on Ephesians 2:8-10.

When the activity begins:
- Divide the class into four groups. Assign to each group one of the stanzas of the hymn.
- The task of each group is to write a paragraph that explains the meaning of the stanza.
- Reassemble and sing the hymn. First, hear the paragraph of explanation, then sing the stanza. Repeat until all stanzas have been sung.
- For a follow-up activity see activity (H) in Dimension 3.

(E) Describe "church" to a visitor from outer space.

Before the session:
- Prepare two instruction sheets.
- Begin sheet 1. Write the following: "GROUP ONE: You are Christians in Ephesus. You have just read the letter being distributed among the churches. Right now, read Ephesians 2:19-22. Talk with each other and decide how you will explain 'church' to someone who has never heard the word. You have five minutes to prepare."

- Begin sheet 2. Write the following: "GROUP TWO: You are aliens from outer space! You have observed a strange ritual. Once every seven days people leave their homes and go to a large building for an hour. Then they depart. You have heard that this is called 'going to church.' What questions would you like to ask these people? Try to think like space aliens! You have five minutes to prepare."
- You may either make one instruction sheet for each group to read aloud or copies so that each person in the group will have a copy of the instructions for his or her group.

TEACHING TIP

This activity is intended to help class members experience the difficulty of communication, given both time and cultural differences. (This is the interpretation problem twentieth and twenty-first century Christians encounter in reading the Bible.)

When the activity begins:
- Divide the class into two groups. Do not tell them who they are. They will discover this when they assemble in their group.
- Give one group "Group 1" instruction sheet(s) and the other group "Group 2" sheet(s).
- At the end of five minutes, announce that the people in Group 1 are first century Christians from Ephesus, and that people in Group 2 are aliens from outer space!
- Ask members to form conversation groups made up of one Christian and one space person. Allow five minutes for these discussions.
- Reassemble and debrief. Both groups were playing unfamiliar roles.
—How difficult was it to move back in time twenty centuries, or away from planet Earth through both time and space?
—Were Christians able to explain church so that space people could understand?

(F) Invite an architect or builder.

Before the session:
- Invite to your class session an architect or a builder.
- Share, in advance, the outline for this activity, which poses six questions: three to the guest and three to the class members.

When the activity begins:
- Ask the guest to talk about a building foundation.
—How is it constructed?
—How important is it?
- Ask the class to number off by two's.
- Ask group 1 to read in their Bibles, 1 Corinthians 3:10-15. Ask group 2 to read Ephesians 2:20-22. Ask:
—Who is the foundation of the church, the "household of God"?

- Ask the guest:
—What is the purpose of a cornerstone? In modern construction is this stone still used as a point of reference for aligning the walls?
- Ask the class:
—How can Christ be said to be the cornerstone of the church, or the "household of God"?
- Ask the guest:
—A footnote in the NRSV indicates that "cornerstone" in this passage may also be read "keystone."
—What is a keystone, and how important is this in construction?
- Ask the class:
—How can Christ be said to be the keystone of the church or the "household of God"?

(G) Pantomime some results of Christ's death.

Three images are used by the writer of Ephesians to talk about what has been accomplished through the death of Christ.
- Divide the class into three groups.
- Give groups five minutes to plan.
—Group 1 will plan to pantomime the breaking down of the wall of hostility between Jews and Gentiles.
—Group 2 will plan to pantomime the reconciliation of the Jews and Gentiles with God, and with each other.
—Group 3 will plan to pantomime the image of "one humanity in Christ."
- Introduce the pantomimes by reading Ephesians 2:14-17.
- After this reading, let groups present their pantomimes in order, beginning with Group 1. There should be no talking, and the transition from one presentation to the next should be as smooth as possible.
- The class may choose to repeat the pantomime sequence, using the first as the practice run.

Dimension 3: What Does the Bible Mean to Us?

(H) Continue hymn study.

If you chose activity (D) in Dimension 2, you may want to continue with this activity.
- Divide once again into four groups.
- Assign each stanza of the hymn to one of the four groups, but not to the group that worked with it in activity (C).
- The task of each group is to answer the question, "What does this stanza mean to us today?"
- Hear reports from groups.

(I) Share personal experiences of "resurrection."

The writer of Ephesians uses the metaphor of Jesus' death and resurrection to affirm that through Christ believers have been "resurrected" from their old way of life (Ephesians 2:4-6).
• Give opportunity for class members to share briefly times in their lives when they have been able to make new beginnings.
• Indicate a time allotment of two minutes. Responses may include, for example, changing of habits, attitudes, self-understanding, lifestyle, vocation, or faith commitments. Give opportunity, but do not push! No response is wrong.

(J) Rewrite the "household code" in Ephesians.

It is difficult to apply the household code in Ephesians to family life in twentieth and twenty-first century United States. Few families have servants or slaves. In 1993 thirty percent of the families with children under eighteen years of age were headed by only one parent, almost always the mother.
• Think with your class about family life today.
• Examine the expectations of Ephesians 5:21–6:9. (See the article "A Household Code" in the Additional Bible Helps section at the end of this session.) Ask:
—How would your class write a "household code" for Christian families today? You may want to divide into groups of three or four persons for the initial discussion.

(K) Identify ways to praise God.

Before the session, provide paper and pencils.
• Say to the group:
—The last paragraph of the study book is tantalizing! There are no easy answers here. If the church exists, fundamentally for the praise of God, what does that mean? Here, again, there are many right answers, although none may be called definitive.
• Challenge the class to brainstorm. (Brainstorming means that ideas can be suggested "off the top of the head" without having to defend them. They are neither right nor wrong, just flashes of insight that must later be tested.)
• Instruct each person to write in two minutes as many ways as they can think of in which to praise God.
• List these on chalkboard or a large sheet of paper. Each person should give only one idea until everyone has had a chance to contribute to the list. Continue around the group until all ideas have been listed.
• Can the class begin to group these ideas into categories?
• Consider:

—Are some ways of praising God more important to us than others?
—Or, are some more important to God?

(L) Write it down.

If the summarizing questions in session 4, activity (K) seem to have been helpful, suggest them again for this session. Read thoughts in personal notebooks.

Additional Bible Helps

The City of Ephesus

The city of Ephesus lies at the mouth of the Cayster River that flows into the Aegean Sea. It was first colonized about 1000 B.C. by Ionian Greeks. It was the site of a primitive shrine to the Mother Goddess, an ancient fertility deity. The Greeks identified her with their own goddess, Artemis.

In 560 B.C. the city moved and in later years was under the rule of Lydia, then Persia, and in 334 B.C., Greece with the arrival of Alexander. To avoid flooding it was moved again in 286 B.C., this time to higher ground. Finally, in 133 B.C. it was once more under the rule of Rome.

During the time of Paul, Ephesus was the fourth largest city in the Roman Empire and the capital of the Roman province known as "Asia."

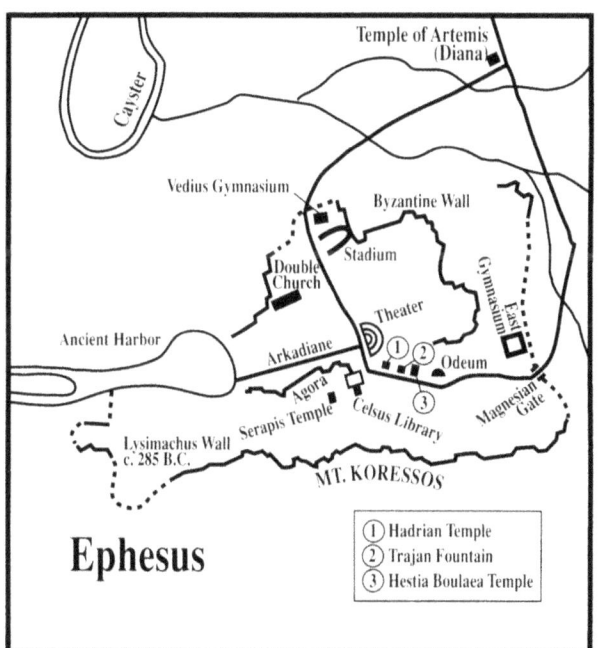

The Letter

The Letter to the Ephesians is probably a general letter, not specifically to the church at Ephesus. Historically it has been addressed in several ways. The first indication that it was addressed to the Ephesians is by Irenaeus about A.D. 180.

Earlier, in a collection of Paul's letters edited by Marcion, the letter was addressed "To the Laodiceans." The most reliable manuscripts do not include any place name in Ephesians 1:1. Nor does the letter give any indication of the place from which it was written.

Most biblical scholars agree that this is not an authentic "Pauline" letter, but one dating from a later period, probably around A.D. 80-95. Evidence from the letter itself is cited to support this determination. These following items might be mentioned, in addition to the ones cited in the study book. (See "The Special Character of Ephesians.")

1. The concept of sin differs from that found in other Pauline letters. It is no longer viewed in the singular, as "Sin," a hostile power, but now refers to individual behaviors, as in "sins."

2. The waiting seems to be over, and believers are now already raised up, and seated with Christ in heavenly places. (See Ephesians 2:6.)

3. The status of women has diminished. Here is contained the oft-quoted passage that reinforces the hierarchy of relationships. "Wives, be subject to your husbands. . .for the husband is the head of the wife just as Christ is the head of the church. . ." (Ephesians 5:22-24). Nowhere do the undisputed Pauline letters call for the subjection of wives to their husbands.

The Whole Armor of God

Ephesians 6:10-17 describes desired human qualities with a military image found in Isaiah 11:5—the "armor of God." In Isaiah the imagery is used to show how God will use force against God's enemies. When "armor of God" is used by the writer of Ephesians, however, it intends to describe how humanity will be able to withstand the temptations of evil.

The "whole armor of God" is composed of truth, righteousness, faith, salvation, the spirit of God, and readiness to proclaim the gospel. The "weapons" are not virtues that humanity can create for itself, but their source is rooted in the power of God.

While this same imagery from Isaiah is used by Paul in 1 Thessalonians 5:8, its use there is more characteristic of Paul than that used by the writer of Ephesians. In 1 Thessalonians 5:8 Paul urged the reader to put on the "breastplate of faith and love," as well as a helmet, which is the "hope of salvation."

This contrasts with the writer of Ephesians who cites the "helmet of salvation" (omitting *hope*), and does not include anywhere the rest of the Pauline triad, faith and love. In Ephesians salvation is assumed to be an accomplished fact. In 1 Thessalonians Paul thinks of salvation as something for which one longs and which is to be received at a later date.

A Household Code

A household, as understood in the New Testament, consisted of more than father, mother, children, and perhaps extended family members. It also included servants, slaves, and their family members. There needed to be some way to regulate the complex relationships that existed among such a diverse and often large household. As a result, summary lists of responsibilities were developed. One such list is found in Ephesians 5:21–6:9. A similar one is present in Colossians 3:18–4:1. Since the time of Martin Luther these responsibilities have often been described as "household codes." Such lists did not originate with first century Christians. Precedent can be found in Jewish, Greek, and Roman cultures. For example, the Ten Commandments in the Old Testament served this same regulatory function. Elements often found in the "household codes" were these:

—In everything, a wife should be subject to her husband (Ephesians 5:22-24).
—A husband should love his wife, as he does his own body (Ephesians 5:25-33).
—A wife should respect her husband (Ephesians 5:33).
—Children should obey their parents (Ephesians 6:1-3).
—Fathers should "bring up" their children "in the discipline and instruction of the Lord" (Ephesians 6:4).
—Slaves should obey their masters (Ephesians 6:5-8).
—Masters should not threaten their slaves (Ephesians 6:9).

It is important to note, however, that the code in Ephesians does not begin with verse 22 of chapter 5, but with verse 21 which says, "Be subject to one another out of reverence for Christ." The footnote to this verse in the *HarperCollins Study Bible: NRSV* (HarperCollins, 1993) makes an observation and raises a question. The observation: While the rest of the code may be rooted in earlier traditions, verse 21 seems to be original with the writer of Ephesians. The question: *Is this admonition directed to all persons in the household or is it primarily addressed to the relationship between spouses?* In either case, in terms of "real life," what does this verse mean?

13

Philippians 1:27–2:13

One Name Above All

LEARNING MENU

On the basis of what you know about your class members, their needs, and the ways in which they learn best, choose at least one learning activity from each of the three Dimensions.

Opening Prayer
God our creator,
yours is the morning and yours is the evening.
Let Christ the sun of righteousness
shine forever in our hearts
and draw us to that light
where you live in radiant glory.
We ask this for the sake of Jesus Christ our Redeemer. Amen.

(From *Book of Common Worship*, © 1993 Westminster/John Knox Press; page 501. Used by permission of Westminster/John Knox Press.)

Dimension 1: What Does the Bible Say?

(A) Answer Dimension 1 questions.

Answers to questions in the study book include the following:
 1. God granted the Philippians two privileges: believing in Christ and suffering for Christ.

 2. The Philippians could fill Paul with joy by being of one mind, one love, and in full accord with each other (2:2).

 3. In Philippians 2:6-8 Christ was described as having emptied himself, taken on human form, and humbled himself, becoming obedient even to death on the cross.

 4. In Philippians 2:9-11 God is described as having exalted Jesus and given him a name above all names so that everyone will confess that Jesus Christ is Lord to the glory of God.

(B) Hear a letter from Paul.

Paul's letters were written to be read aloud as Christians gathered for worship. This must have taken patience on the part of worshipers, for even though Paul's letters are some of the shorter books in the Bible, reading aloud consumes a great deal of time.

- Help students experience what this reading must have been like. Several days before the class session recruit someone who will be the reader of one of Paul's letters.
- The reader will read aloud Philippians 4:10-23, sometimes identified as a separate letter.
- Discuss:
—How do class members describe the style of this passage?
- *Harper's Bible Commentary* uses the word *delicate*. Use the information in this commentary as a basis for a class discussion of "style."

Dimension 2: What Does the Bible Mean?

(C) Find athletic images in Paul's letters.

Before the session:
- Write these references on chalkboard or a large sheet of paper: Philippians 1:30; 2:16; 3:13-14; 4:3; 1 Corinthians 9:24-27; Galatians 2:2; 5:7. Note that Paul sometimes used athletic images as he described the way Christians should meet life's challenges.

When the activity begins:
- Invite class members to find these verses in their Bibles. Have them read aloud.
- Discuss:
—What feelings are evoked when describing life's journey as an athletic event?
—What other metaphors characteristic of contemporary life might be used?

(D) Sing hymns about "the Name above all."

Throughout the centuries hymns have been written about "the name of Jesus." If the class enjoys singing, you could conclude this unit of study with a "hymn sing through the centuries" of hymns based on Philippians 2:6-11.
- Choose one, or all, of the following:
—Ninth century, "Creator of the Stars of Night" (*The United Methodist Hymnal*, No. 692);
—Eighteenth century, "Jesus! the Name High Over All" (No. 193);
—Nineteenth century, "Precious Name" (No. 536);
—Twentieth century, "There's Something About That Name" (No. 171).

(E) Explore four themes.

Before the session:
- Prepare four large sheets of paper as illustrated below:
  (1) Suffering, 1:29
  (2) Unity, 1:27; 2:2, 5
  (3) Others, 2:3-4
  (4) Salvation, 2:12
  The author of the study book cautions against misunderstanding these four passages.

When the activity begins:
- Instruct members to find and read the first reference.

—What did Paul mean?
- Summarize the discussion on a large sheet of paper.
- Follow the same procedure with the other three references.
- Follow this activity, if you wish, with activity (G).

Dimension 3: What Does the Bible Mean to Us?

(F) Question the concept of "regard for others."

TEACHING TIP
Philippians 2:1-4 has become a controversial passage for persons who are oppressed by the inequalities of a social system. It seems to honor submission and discourage assertiveness. This activity will engage the class in a discussion of this dilemma.

- Divide the class into two groupings for conversation.
- Ask group 1 to read the biblical reference, Philippians 2:1-4, and be prepared to share their understanding of what it means for Christians today.
- Ask group 2 to read in the study book, Dimension 3, page 106 where the author cautions against misinterpreting Paul, and prepare to report to the large group.
- Reassemble the class.
- Explore:
—What does group 1 say that this passage means for us today?
—According to group 2, what does the author of the study book say?
—In what ways do the groups agree? Disagree?

(G) Avoid misunderstanding Paul.

TEACHING TIP
This activity may follow activity (E), or it may stand alone. If it is to stand alone, prepare four large sheets of paper according to the illustration in activity (E).

- Divide the class into four groups, each group assigned to the reference on one of the sheets of paper.
- Ask each group to read the numbered section in Dimension 3 of the study book that corresponds with the number on the paper.
- Write a summary on the paper. (If this activity is a follow-up of activity (E) the paper will now contain the meaning found in the passage by the class, as well as the meaning suggested by the author of the study book.)
- Reflect:
—How will the class respond if the meanings are significantly different?

JOURNEY THROUGH THE BIBLE

(H) Reflect on God's "place."

Where is God? Heaven as a place is rooted in an ancient understanding of the universe as composed of three stories, or tiers.

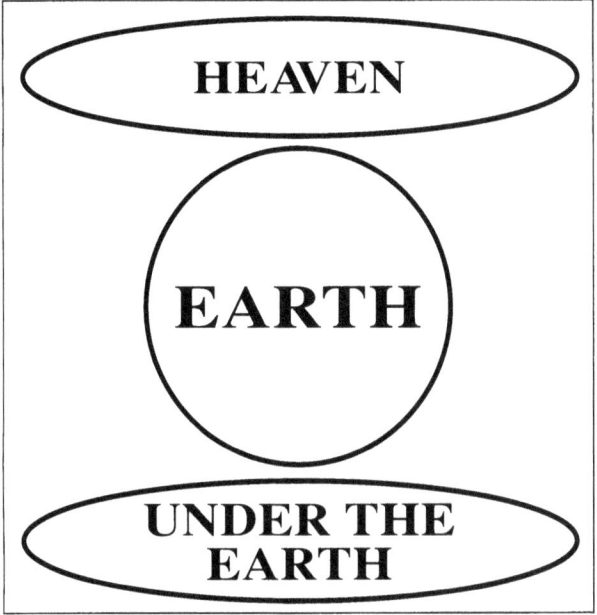

- Consider: Those in our time who have explored outer space have not reported seeing heaven!
—Where is God for us? (No answer is necessarily wrong.)

(I) Listen to selections from Handel's *Messiah*.

- Read in unison the last sentence of the study book, page 108.
- Listen to selections from *Messiah*, especially the soprano solo, "If God Be for Us" followed by the chorus, "Worthy Is the Lamb."
- Experience the difference between a "solo performance" and a full chorus.

(J) Name favorite hymns.

A hymn is more than an intellectual faith statement. The combination of words with music evokes feelings that are as important as the words. This is true of the hymn in Philippians 2:6-11, and it is true of our favorite hymns today.

- Create on chalkboard or a large sheet of paper a format three columns wide.
- Title the first column "Name of Hymn" and list favorite hymns as suggested by class members.
- After the list has been completed, title the second column "Main Idea" and note the main idea of the hymn as recalled by the class. Do not refer to a hymnal for this activity.
- Finally, title the third column, "Main Feeling."

—Go through the list of hymns and define the feelings evoked by each hymn. (They may have little or nothing to do with the main idea.)

(K) Write a letter from prison.

Is Philippians the kind of letter your class would write if they suddenly found themselves in prison?

- Describe this scenario:
  The class decided to stage a peaceful protest outside of the county jail over what was perceived to be the unjust incarceration of a member of the church. The entire class was arrested for "disturbing the peace." Everyone went to jail. The expected release did not happen. With no release date in sight everyone was given the opportunity to write a letter to their church.
- Discuss:
—What would you say in the letter?
—Would it be anything like Paul's letter to the Philippians?
—If your letter would not be like Paul's, why was not Paul's letter like yours?

TEACHING TIPS
Summarizing Activities

This session concludes a unit that has stressed ideas more than actions or human interest stories. It will be important to spend time in summarizing so that class members can leave this study with some clear ideas about the early church and its ministry. It will also be important for them to have a sense of the relevance of Paul for twentieth and twenty-first century Christians. Activities (L), (M), and (N) are intended to aid in this process. Each of them suggests writing on large sheets of paper so that the organization of this unit will be visual as well as mental.

Unless the class is very large, everyone can participate in these summarizing activities without dividing into groups. This way no one will miss anything.

(L) Recall Paul.

Give serious thought to choosing this activity. This session concludes the study of Paul's most important letters, as well as the Letter to the Ephesians, whose authorship is in doubt.

- Use a large sheet of paper with these *who*, *what*, *when*, and *where* questions as a basis for this summary.
- Who was Paul?
—List everything that can be recalled about Paul as a person.
- Who were Paul's co-workers?
—Recall men, women and the roles they played in Paul's ministry.
- Who was Paul's audience?

—How did his "audience" differ from that of the apostles located in Jerusalem?
• Where was Paul's ministry?
—Use a map to locate Rome, Galatia, Ephesus, Corinth, Philippi, as well as other locations associated with Paul.
• When were the letters in this unit written?
—See commentaries or study Bibles.
• What were Paul's major accomplishments? This question should elicit some interesting discussion.
• What was Paul's major message?
—What were the themes of his letters?
—How did he see himself as different from other preachers of the gospel?

TEACHING TIP

This activity as a summary can stand alone. It may also be followed by a combination of activities (M) and (N).

(M) Express personal meanings found in Paul's writings.

For some Paul is the final and authentic interpreter of Christianity; for others, Paul has no relevance for the modern world. Perhaps most Christians are either ambivalent or confused. What new meanings or confusions have resulted from this study for your class members? Have there been any life-changing moments?

• If members have been keeping a notebook after each session they may want to record their feelings now in that book. Give time for this. Ask if people wish to share their thoughts with the class. Do not insist.
• If notebooks have not been used, provide pencil and paper for this activity.
• After five minutes ask if there are those who will share personal meanings they have discovered in this study. Sharing personal meanings is not a requirement.

(N) Think beyond the personal.

• Take the last paragraph of the study book seriously (page 108). Personal meaning discovery leads to personal commitment. But when "soloists" join the "faith chorus," bold new possibilities may emerge.
• Recall some of the themes of this unit.
• Post them so that all can see them. Some of them are listed here:
—The impartiality of God
—God's saving grace
—Freedom for new life
—Jews and Christians in dialogue
—Saving God's earth
—Doing God's will
—Being agents of God's love
—Ethical responsibility
—Being Christian in a pagan context
—Church as the body of Christ

—A "new creation" through Christ
—Reconciliation as a way of life
—Ministry of all believers
—Breaking down walls of hostility
• Consider:
—What could happen in this church if this class took these themes seriously?
—Which of these themes does this church most need to hear?
—Which of these themes does the community of nations need to hear?
—What action can this class take?

(O) Write it down.

As part of activity (L) class members may already have written in their notebooks. If not, encourage them to do so soon.
• Discuss:
—Have members found this activity helpful?
—As a class project will they want to continue it beyond this session?

Additional Bible Helps

The City of Philippi

At the time of Paul, Philippi was a Roman colony in the province of Macedonia. It was located on the Via Egnatia, an important Roman highway that served as one of the key links between Rome and Asia Minor.

Even before the fourth century B.C. there was a city at the site of Philippi. To secure nearby silver and gold mines, Philip II of Macedonia annexed the whole region. In 356 B.C. he named the city after himself. A wall still survives that may have been built 2,400 years ago.

Philippi was a city of many religious influences. There were the worshipers of the Roman gods, Jupiter and Mars; worshipers of the very popular Thracian goddess, Bendis; and a sanctuary for the worship of a Phrygian goddess, Cybele. In the midst of these Roman deities was an established Jewish congregation. To this religious diversity came Paul in about A.D. 50 to found the first European Christian community.

Visitors to the site of Philippi today will no longer find a city, but will see the work of archeologists whose research there continues.

The Letter
There is no doubt that Paul was the writer of this letter to the church at Philippi and that it was written from prison (Philippians 1:7, 13-14). In it Paul expressed a mixture of joy and concern. He rejoiced in the faithfulness of the church at Philippi and at his expectation that they will be saved. He rejoiced that, because of their faithfulness, he would receive a crown. But Paul was also anxious and concerned, warning his readers to beware of false missionaries who preached righteousness based on strict adherence to the law, and who insisted on circumcision.

The date of this letter and the place of writing are two yet unresolved issues. If written from Ephesus, the date should be A.D. 54-55. If written from Caesarea, it should be dated between A.D. 57 and 59. A later date of A.D. 60-61 is likely if written from Rome. A third unresolved issue is a question about the letter itself. Is this one letter or several? While Philippians should probably be read as a single, unified letter, there are scholars who challenge this assumption. They suggest that parts of three separate letters may have been combined to form what has been handed down as one letter.

Who Are the "Dogs"?
Dogs were highly esteemed in Egypt, but perhaps because of their scavenger habits, the Hebrews viewed dogs with utter disgust. When used to refer to people, *dog* became a term of extreme contempt, sometimes used by Jews to refer to non-Jews.

As Paul wrote Philippians 3:2, there can be little doubt about his mood—he was on the attack. On the heels of a reasoned discussion about his co-workers, Timothy and Epaphroditus, he launched into an impassioned warning: "Beware of the dogs, beware of the evil workers, beware of those who mutilate the flesh!" All of these references probably point to the same group of people, perhaps those whom he referred to in 2 Corinthians 11:13 as "false apostles." Although there can be no certainty about their identity, it is safe to assume that Paul was referring to other missionaries preaching in the same region but who were preaching in contradiction to certain of his own convictions. Some suggest that these "false apostles" may have been Judaizers, those Gentiles who insisted that to be Christian one must live as a Jew, which included the necessity of circumcision. Others suggest that they may have been gnostics, with an emphasis on the union of the "self" with a transcendent, creator God. Still others speculate that they may have been Jewish-Christian missionaries, who in addition to preaching the need for circumcision, placed a high value on their own extraordinary religious status.

The Philippians' Generosity
Paul wrote this letter to the church at Philippi, a group of Christians who had a history of providing money for his mission. (When Paul spoke of the Macedonians, it can be assumed that this reference included the Christians in Philippi.) Although themselves poor, they paid their commitment to the offering for the poor of Jerusalem.

Early in his ministry, when Paul left Macedonia, the Philippians were the only ones who gave money for his support. They may have sent it with Silvanus and Timothy (Philippians 4:15). Even before he left Macedonia, when he was in Thessalonica, they sent money to him "more than once" (Philippians 4:16). Then, while he was once again in prison, they again sent money, this time with Epaphroditus (Philippians 4:18).

In addition to showing Paul's gratitude to the Philippians for their generosity, this "thank you" letter also revealed Paul's need to feel independent. He expressed joy that they had finally sent him some financial support ("I rejoice in the Lord greatly that now at last you have revived your concern for me. . . " 4:10). In almost the next breath, however, he wanted to reassure them that he was "not . . . referring to being in need." This was followed almost immediately by his own acknowledgment of his need: "In any case, it was kind of you to share my distress" (4:14).

Connected to One Another

By Maryann J. Dotts

One of the current mental health problems in our country is loneliness. How incredible that seems when we can call by phone from our offices, cars, or planes, and when we can fly to almost any place in a few hours! Have we lost our basic ability to be in community, to be connected? As teachers and learners in adult classes, we need to ask ourselves if our classes provide opportunities for community, for knowing and being known.

Broken Connections—An Old Problem

After Jesus died, the first disciples were lonely, bewildered, and afraid. Their dreams were shattered. How could this happen to those with whom Jesus had entrusted his teachings?

When the full impact of Jesus' death registered, the disciples experienced a variety of emotions. They needed time: Time to work through their grief, to understand what their role would now be. Time to lean on one another, to comfort one another. Time to rest and regroup, to renew their energy for carrying the message to all of the world.

They needed assurance: Assurance that it was safe to go into the world where their leader had been brutally killed. Assurance that they could proclaim the good news of Jesus, regardless of the fact that they had been laborers and business men, not trained religious leaders.

Acts 2 records how this small band of disciples spent the time they needed and discovered through God's Spirit the assurance they needed. When the disciples left the upper room, they were empowered to preach. Thousands of people responded by connecting with this new religious group in caring ways.

Like the early disciples, we each have experienced times when we needed to be still, needed to take time to be nourished for the tasks ahead. We have needed to share our situation with others and to experience the ways we are connected to one another. We have needed to discover that we were indeed revitalized for the tasks at hand.

Organize for Community

This connectedness or community building should be an intentional aspect of every adult class and group in our congregations. We should give class members opportunities to evaluate the class organization, traditions, projects, and concerns to see if this basic need of being known or connected is experienced in the group. We should ask for suggestions to improve the class organization.

To be realistic, we can only maintain four or five close relationships at one time (including our family members). Therefore we should not expect to know everyone in the class, but we can expect to know one or two class members well.

The following strategies will promote a sense of connection between class members:

- Plan a time for fellowship. Designate a greeter to meet people at the door. Allow class members at least ten minutes to move around and speak to several persons. Provide refreshment.
- Involve many persons in small manageable responsibilities. Ask for volunteers to make, serve, and clean up refreshments. As a class, elect ministers of encouragement. Appoint a social committee to plan and publicize regular class gatherings.
- Ask each person present to introduce himself or herself each week, especially if the class is large or visitors are present. Or provide name tags each week.
- Take time each week for prayer requests, announcements of birthdays, anniversaries, and special honors.
- Create a prayer chain by dividing the class into groups of

ten. Give each class member a copy of the names and phone numbers for their prayer chain group. When prayers are needed, the class president, teacher, or other volunteer calls the first person on each prayer chain list. That person calls the next person on the list, and so on.
- Print a directory of class members' names, addresses, phone numbers, and birthdays.
- Draw names for prayer partners or secret pals for a stated period of time, such as during Advent, Lent, or the summer months. Secret pals can be revealed at the end of the specified period of time and new names drawn. New prayer partners may also be paired on a regular basis.

Encourage Variety

Our classes are filled with persons of different experiences, life situations, education, and opinions. When we acknowledge and respect one another's differences, we help persons to feel accepted and connected with class members. When we encourage conformity, we automatically exclude some persons.

When we teach, we can encourage sharing different opinions. We must recognize that class members will have had varied religious backgrounds and will have varied interpretations of Scripture, church doctrine, and contemporary issues. Our responses to diversity can set the tone for the class and will either create an atmosphere of hospitality or project a lack of welcome.

At Pentecost there were many voices heard, and we need to keep an open accepting approach to our class discussions and activities. There is a place for all our gifts in caring for others. God has created us for community. Our adult classes can be part of the delivery system of God's love. The challenge is how we can bring more shared time into the lives of our busy class members.

Maryann J. Dotts is a Christian educator and freelance writer who lives in Florida.

From Teacher in the Church Today, *May 1992, pages 30-31. Copyright © 1992 by Cokesbury.*

Paul Speaks to "Sensible People"

Paul Speaks to "Sensible People"

Paul composed his letters and framed his arguments with considerable care. This accords with his purpose for writing, which was to inform, instruct, explain, and persuade. He defined and sought to clarify issues; he reasoned things out. He also anticipated objections and developed counter-arguments (note 2 Corinthians 10:4-5). As a rule, he did not just make assertions; he also made an effort to show why his assertions were correct. He was generally not content simply to cite Scripture; he usually interpreted or argued from them. He hoped that his readers would be able to follow his reasoning; and so he wrote, for example, "I am speaking as to sensible people; you yourselves judge what I say" (1 Corinthians 10:15; compare 14:6-11; 2 Corinthians 5:13; Philippians 3:15; 4:8). And again, "We write you nothing other than what you can . . . understand; I hope that you will understand . . ." (2 Corinthians 1:13).

There was no one in the first century church, to our knowledge, who was so deliberate as Paul about lifting the truth claims of the gospel to the level of understanding. Apart from this, to cite but one example, there could have been no effective missionary proclamation, least of all among the Gentiles. In fact, apart from Paul's efforts, there might have been no lasting Gentile mission at all. It was Paul's speaking of the truth of the gospel, as he understood it, that provided the clearest and surest foundation for such a mission. His vision of God's impartiality, as he saw that to be disclosed in Christ, led him to affirm that Jews and Gentiles have equal standing with God. (See Romans 3:29-30; and compare with 15:8-12). Therefore, a mission to the Gentiles was not simply authorized but required (1 Corinthians 9:16). He also saw that this interpretation raised serious questions about God's election of Israel and about the role of the law within God's saving purpose. He sought to answer these questions.

If Paul still catches our attention, it is not because he is or ever can be fully understood. It is partly because his labors and letters have had such an impact on the history of Christianity. Primarily he still commands attention because in his letters he examines with extraordinary insight the ordinary relationships and events of people's lives. He struggles with basic questions about human existence that are common to every age.

Finally, the task of understanding Paul is one of engaging his thought and considering how it may challenge and give clarity to our own lives.

The Women in Paul's Letters

Some passages in letters ascribed to Paul have been used to silence the voices of women in today's church and to minimize their influence in the workings of the church. These passages, however, do not support a view of Paul as one opposed to the leadership of women. On the contrary, his letters give evidence that women played a significant role in the early history of the church and that they were recognized by Paul as able co-workers. There are more than a dozen such women mentioned by name in Paul's letters. Five of them are noted here:

Phoebe

Phoebe was a member of the church at Cenchreae, a seaport town near Corinth. It is quite possible that she owned the house in which the Cenchreae house church met. Paul called her a benefactor of many, including himself, which suggests that she was a person of wealth and power. In referring to her as *diakonos* Paul also described her as a minister or as one who had special responsibilities in the church. It is disappointing that there is no further description of her specific duties. In Romans 16:1-2 Paul commended her as a leader worthy to be assisted and asked that her leadership be respected. Some think that this chapter may have been a letter sent to Ephesus rather than the church in Rome, on the occasion of her move from Cenchreae to Ephesus. In any case, it is clear that Paul thought highly of her and of her work.

Priscilla (Prisca)

The woman probably closest to Paul was Priscilla, whom

he referred to by using the familiar form, "Prisca." She was married to Aquila, a Jewish convert to Christianity and a tentmaker. Originally from Rome, they were probably among those Jewish leaders exiled to Corinth during the reign of Claudius. They established house churches in Rome, Corinth, and Ephesus and may have the distinction of being the first married couple to lead a congregation! Paul was their house guest for a number of months while they lived in Corinth. Six times they are mentioned, with Prisca's name preceding Aquila's in four of these times. This may indicate that she had inherited wealth, or that she had a higher social status than Aquila. It may also reflect Paul's recognition of her as having made a major contribution to his ministry.

The writer of Acts depicted these two friends of Paul as assertive and fearless when it came to their understanding of the gospel. Acts 18:24-26 describes an occasion in Ephesus when they heard the famous and eloquent Apollos preach in the synagogue. According to this account, "Priscilla and Aquila . . . took him aside and explained the Way of God to him more accurately." Priscilla was not a "silent woman."

Paul made a tantalizing reference in Romans 16:3-4 to Prisca and Aquila as ones who "risked their necks for my life." This may acknowledge a long period of devoted and arduous work on behalf of his ministry, or it may be a reference to some dramatic event that Paul simply did not record.

Euodia and Syntyche

The entire known story about these two women occurs in two verses, Philippians 4:2-3. They were leaders in the church at Philippi who worked side by side with each other and with Paul. They were not recent recruits to the work of the gospel, but may be some of the ones longest with the congregation. Verse 3 suggests that others with whom they have worked were now dead. However, these two women do not find mention in Paul's letter because of their hard and loyal work, but because they had some kind of an argument. There is no clue as to the nature of this falling out. Whether it was his concern for the personal relationship or his concern for the welfare of the church that may have been disrupted by this argument between two of its leaders, we cannot be sure. What we do know is that Paul considered it serious enough to call upon a third party (the "yokefellow") to help these two women settle their dispute.

Chloe

Chloe, perhaps the leader of a house church, was famous only for having sent a message to Paul. She knew about the disagreements and upheavals within the church at Corinth and thought that Paul should be aware of this situation also. She sent word to Paul through "her people," who may have been her slaves, her employees, or other household members. Obviously Paul thought her information was reliable, because this matter became the chief theme of a letter to the Corinthian Christians. Where Chloe lived is unclear. She may have been a member of the congregation in Corinth, or she may have resided in Ephesus, the city from which Paul wrote this letter.

The Men in Paul's Letters

Both men and women shared leadership roles in the churches to whom Paul wrote, but his closest associates were Timothy, Titus, Barnabus, and Silvanus. At one time or another each of these men shared with him the rigors of his traveling ministry.

Timothy

Paul referred to Timothy (1 Corinthians 4:17) as "my beloved and faithful child in the Lord. . . ." According to one source, [*Harper's Bible Dictionary*] both Timothy's mother, Eunice, and his grandmother, Lois, were among the faithful. Thus, he could lay claim to being a third generation Christian. This same source notes that Eunice was a Jew, married to a Gentile.

When Paul first met Timothy is unclear. The writer of Acts (16:1-3) recorded a meeting at the time of Paul's visit to Derbe and Lystra when Timothy was already a disciple.

Timothy accompanied Paul and Silvanus on missions to Thessalonica and Corinth as a trusted colleague, and later was sent back to Thessalonica by himself as Paul's personal emissary. Although some biblical interpreters have implied that Paul may have been unwise to trust a relatively inexperienced young man with such a mission, it is clear that Paul had complete confidence in him. He later sent Timothy to Corinth, a church that was in the midst of division and troubling times, as his personal representative. In Philippians 2:19-24 he expressed complete confidence in Timothy using phrases such as: "I have no one like him who will be genuinely concerned for your welfare . . . Timothy's worth you know, how like a son with a father he has served with me in the work of the gospel." The letters known as 1 and 2 Timothy are addressed to "Timothy, my beloved child." Scholars today, however, do not now consider these to be authentic letters from the pen of Paul, but writings dating between A.D. 90-110 by an unknown author, who used Paul's name to add credibility to his own words.

Titus

Titus was a Gentile of Greek origin, an associate whom Paul looked upon as crucial to his ministry. When Paul went to Jerusalem following his call to be an apostle to the Gentiles, he took with him Titus and Barnabas (Galatians 2:1). It is likely that Titus continued with Paul during his extended ministry in Ephesus. He was the bearer of at least one of Paul's letters to the church at Corinth, probably the one known as the "letter of tears." (See more on this in

Sessions 5-8.) One of his important responsibilities was to encourage the Corinthian church to fulfill its pledge to a collection that Paul was taking up for the Jewish Christians in Jerusalem.

Like the two letters purportedly written by Paul to Timothy, the Letter to Titus is undoubtedly from the hand of a later author. These three letters have come to be known as the Pastoral Epistles.

Barnabas

Barnabas was a Levite from Cyprus, whose actual name, according to Acts 4:36, was Joseph. It is said that the apostles named him "Barnabas," a Hebrew name meaning "son of encouragement." He was a Diaspora Jew, one born in a country outside of Palestine. When Paul journeyed to Jerusalem, accompanied by Barnabas and Silvanus, he sought to make contact with the disciples there. Because of Paul's earlier persecution of the followers of Jesus, it was understandable when the disciples were a bit cautious. However, Barnabas was known and trusted by the disciples, so he was able to act as intermediary on Paul's behalf.

Much of our information about the association of Paul and Barnabas comes from the writer of Acts. If this material is accurate, Barnabas and Paul engaged side by side in many missions. They worked together in Syria-Cilicia; they took a famine offering to Jerusalem from the Christians in Antioch; together they undertook a mission to Cyprus and the Iconium region of Asia Minor; and together they attended a conference in Jerusalem.

Eventually, however, they went their separate ways. Their disagreement, in part, involved John Mark, the cousin of Barnabas. Apparently John Mark had accompanied them on an earlier mission but had left the mission early. This early leave taking did not sit well with Paul; so when another tour was planned, Paul was reluctant to allow him to go. Nevertheless, the years in the company of Barnabas were theologically formative ones for Paul, and Barnabas may have been a contributing factor.

It has been suggested by some scholars that Barnabas wrote The Letter to the Hebrews, although there is no real evidence to support this speculation.

Silvanus

Silvanus is probably the person referred to in the Book of Acts as "Silas." When Paul and Barnabas separated, Paul chose Silvanus to accompany him on a mission to Asia Minor, Macedonia, and Achaia. If Silvanus was in fact a Roman citizen, as Acts reports, that could have been a help to Paul as they journeyed through the cities of the Roman Empire. In 2 Corinthians 1:19 there is indication that Silvanus, along with Timothy, accompanied him on a visit to the church at Corinth. There is also evidence that he may have stayed on in Macedonia when Paul continued on his journey.

Paul as a Letter Writer

Our knowledge of the early Christian church from Christian sources would be almost nonexistent without the letters of Paul. Before the writing of the four Gospels and before the Book of Acts, there was Paul the letter-writer.

Why Paul Wrote Letters

When Paul wrote a letter he was usually addressing some problem within the church that had been called to his attention. Sometimes the conflict was between individuals in the church, while sometimes it was a conflict between opposing points of view. Not infrequently, Paul was having to defend himself or his views. Whatever the specific reason, it was a way for Paul to keep in contact with the churches and to remind them of his authority in the interpretation of theological issues.

How Paul Wrote and Sent Letters

Computer-written letters with delete buttons for editing and laser printers for speed and clarity of duplication were not even a fantasy in the mind of Paul! Instead, he probably dictated his letters to scribes who wrote them on a rough roll of papyrus with a reed pen. Editing the letter after it was dictated would too difficult, which may account for why the letters sometimes sound a bit disjointed. When the dictation was completed, the scribe would roll the papyrus with writing on the inside, and on the outside would write instructions for delivery. Wealthy persons hired couriers to carry the letters to their destination, while others sent their letters by some trusted traveler. Not only was it necessary for messengers to safely reach the right destination, but sometimes they also were charged with interpretation of the letter. Delicate or sensitive matters might be entirely omitted from the letter to be conveyed orally by the messenger.

How Churches Received Paul's Letters

Paul usually wrote his letters to a particular church and thus addressed a particular set of circumstances. There is reason to believe, however, that these letters were sometimes shared with other Christian communities. Even though Paul communicated through writing, his letters were intended to be read aloud to the assembled congregation. In fact, in the ancient world letters were regarded as one form of conversation so that the personality or the spirit of the writer was interpreted by the reader who transformed the written word into speech.

www.ingramcontent.com/pod-product-compliance
Lightning Source LLC
LaVergne TN
LVHW061316060426
835507LV00019B/2175